The
Transcendental

(1896)

Michael Reiners
Feb. 15, 2019

Apocalyptic Key

C.G. Harrison

ISBN 0-7661-0530-X

Kessinger Publishing's Rare Reprints
Thousands of Scarce and Hard-to-Find Books!

- •
- •
- •
- •
- •
- •
- •
- •
- •
- •
- •
- •
- •
- •
- •
- •
- •
- •

We kindly invite you to view our extensive catalog list at:
http://www.kessinger.net

THE
TRANSCENDENTAL
UNIVERSE

Six Lectures

ON OCCULT SCIENCE, THEOSOPHY, AND THE CATHOLIC FAITH

BY

C. G. HARRISON

SECOND EDITION

LONDON
GEORGE REDWAY
1896

New Psychic Publications

I.

The Story of the Year. A Record of Feasts and Ceremonies. By the Author of " Light on the Path." Imp. 32mo, pp. 56. Cloth, 1s. 6d. net.

II.

A Handbook of Palmistry after the Ancient Methods. By ROSA BAUGHAN. Sixth (Revised) Edition. With 5 Plates. Demy 8vo, pp. 36, paper wrapper. 1s. net.

III.

Anna Kingsford. Her Life, Letters, Diary, and Work. By her Collaborator, EDWARD MAITLAND. Illustrated with Portraits, Views, Facsimiles, &c. 2 vols., demy 8vo, pp. 896. Cloth, 31s. 6d. net.

IV.

Miracles and Modern Spiritualism. Three Essays by ALFRED RUSSEL WALLACE, D.C.L., LL.D., F.R.S. New Revised Edition, with Chapters on Phantasms and Apparitions. Crown 8vo, pp. 296. Cloth, 5s. net.

V.

The Great Secret and its Unfoldment in Occultism. A Record of Forty Years' Experience in the Modern Mystery. By a Church of England Clergyman. Crown 8vo, pp. 320. Cloth, 5s. net.

VI.

Neo-Platonism. Porphyry the Philosopher to his Wife Marcella. Now First Translated into English by ALICE ZIMMERN, with Preface by RICHARD GARNETT, C.B., LL.D. Crown 8vo. Frontispiece. Cloth, 3s. 6d. net.

PUBLISHED BY

GEORGE REDWAY, 9 HART STREET

BLOOMSBURY

PREFACE.

THE following Lectures were delivered early in 1893 before
the "Berean Society," of which the lecturer had the honour
of being president for the year. It was an association of
students of theoretical occultism, and derived its name from
Acts xvii. 11, which was considered appropriate as indicat-
ing, not so much the nature, as the direction of their studies.
At the request of several who were unable to attend the
Lectures regularly, they are now published in book form.
Their object was to supply materials whereby the true
"Gnosis" may be distinguished from the "oppositions of
science falsely so-called" (ψευδωνύμου γνώσεως), and they
were prepared with special reference to the difficulties which
many find in reconciling the truths brought to light by the
Theosophical Society with the fundamental doctrines of
Christianity; difficulties which frequently arise from an imperfect grasp, on the one hand, of the occult facts, and on
the other, from insufficient acquaintance with the philosophical literature of the Church. The first Lecture deals
with the conflict "behind the veil" which led to the formation of the Theosophical Society, and the subsequent ones
are devoted to an examination of the Theosophical teachings
in regard to man's origin and destiny, and the problem of
evil in the light of occult science. Little alteration has been
made in their form, except that portions of Lecture I. have
been excised, and appear more appropriately in the shape

of an Introduction, which was necessary for the general reader, in whom an intimate knowledge of the aims and methods of the Theosophical Society must not be assumed, when even learned Professors make a boast in the *Nineteenth Century* of being totally unacquainted with its literature, though fully prepared to write articles on the subject.

In giving these Lectures to the public, the author ventures to anticipate a possible criticism. Originally delivered, to a certain extent, *ad clerum*, it may be fairly objected that their style is too dogmatic, and that much is required to be taken for granted which ought to be proved. To answer this objection satisfactorily would be to write an elementary treatise on the methods of occult research, but it may be pointed out that, in occult science, the *deductive* method is employed in discovery, and the *inductive* for proof; and that the data, on which the general truths are founded, are the results of experience in an altogether transcendental region of perception, and in the very nature of things, highly esoteric. The author makes no pretensions to authority in dealing with these the spiritual or "Higher Mysteries," but claims, in virtue of actual knowledge, acquired by the recognised occult methods, the right to instruct in the intellectual or "Lower Mysteries" all those who are willing to accept provisionally certain abstract propositions which are of the nature of general truths not in themselves difficult of comprehension. To these the inductive method may be applied when the learner shall have acquired sufficient knowledge to enable him to synthetise the results of the deductive method, and bring them to the test of experience by comparing and ascertaining their points of contact with the facts of modern science, and the light they throw on the history of mankind.

For the rest, the thanks of the author are due to all "whom it may concern" for the generous aid he has received in the difficult task of translating into intellectual terms that which he but dimly perceives through a very imperfectly developed higher faculty, from those who see more clearly and are able to penetrate the intellectual mists that darken the spiritual heavens; especially since he has not always been able to agree with them on the question of how much it is prudent to reveal, and the advisability of strict adherence to the rule which prohibits the writing down of occult formulæ—a rule which, though it may have had its uses in the past, is practically obsolete, and can only be maintained, in the present day, at great inconvenience. For reasons which will appear, he wishes to make it understood that, in lifting a corner of the veil which has hitherto shrouded the mysteries of the Universe of Causes from all but the initiated, he is acting solely on his own responsibility, and considers himself sufficiently justified by the fact that others have taken advantage of this lack of knowledge on the part of the uninitiated majority to impose on earnest and thinking people a new and false religion with specious pretensions to Catholicity. If "a little knowledge is a dangerous thing," the remedy is surely, not ignorance, but more knowledge.

CONTENTS.

INTRODUCTION.

CONTENTS.

———

APPENDIX.

INTRODUCTION.

THE latter half of the century which is now drawing towards its close has been eminently a period of unrest. In all departments of human activity—in politics, in science and religion—principles, formerly accepted without question as fundamental, have been thrown down into the arena of controversy and subjected to a rigorous examination. And the results of this sifting process are a profound discontent, a restless chafing at the bounds of our present knowledge, which find expression in, and are peculiarly characteristic of the art of the period. " Light, more light !" were the dying words of Goethe, the pioneer of the nineteenth century, and the dying century re-echoes them.

Nothing is more remarkable than the change which has come over our habits of thought within the last few years. Until quite recently, it was considered a sign of intellectual superiority to rest content with the position of an " Agnostic " in regard to the most important subjects which can engage the attention of man. It was asserted that not only do we not know anything about God, the soul, or a future life, but that it is idle to enquire—that true wisdom consists in denial of the possibility of any such knowledge, and that every revelation which professes to

give information on these subjects is the product of a
distempered fancy. But this curious form of intellectual pride led the Agnostics, like the Puritans in
Hudibras, to

> " Compound for sins they were inclined to,
>   By damning those they had no mind to,"

and did not hinder them from indulging in the wildest
speculations about the origin of life on the planet and
gravely asserting that the chief difference between a
man and a monkey is that phosphorus is present in
larger quantities in the brain of the former.

It was inevitable that the pendulum should swing
back in the opposite direction, and the reaction from
Agnosticism has resulted in a very strange phenomenon—the recrudescence of Gnosticism, a veritable
revival of Alexandrian thought in the nineteenth
century.

The Theosophical Movement, or the Gnostic Revival, is a very remarkable one, and deserves to be
treated seriously. It is not to be disposed of by a
few cheap sneers at " Koot-Hoomi " and duplicated
teacups, nor can the number of its adherents be satisfactorily accounted for on the grounds of human
credulity. The majority of people may, or may not,
be fools, but the ranks of the Theosophists are not
recruited from the majority, or the unthinking portion
of the community. The great strength of Theosophy

lies in the fact that it is a coherent system. It is a cosmogony, a philosophy, and a religion ; it claims to possess the key to problems of life and mind which have been regarded hitherto as insoluble ; to account for the religious instinct in man, and to interpret, by the law of evolution, the various forms in which it finds expression in different races of men and at different periods of the world's history.

There are many indications that the age is rapidly out-growing its religious and scientific bands. The swaddling clothes of mechanical authority in religion and the inductive method in science are felt to be a hindrance to its free development, and, if proof be required of this tendency, it is only necessary to refer, on the one hand, to " Lux Mundi," which, as the production of avowed " High " Churchmen, is a remarkable sign of the times, and, on the other, to Professor Crookes' Birmingham Address on the " Genesis of the Elements," in which it would almost seem as if the chasm between " exact science " and the " superstitions of the past " were about to be bridged over, and the Caduceus of Hermes once more adopted as the symbol of creative intelligence.

Ever since the Emperor Justinian struck his " threefold blow at the past," as Bishop Westcott says, viz., when he abolished the Consulship at Rome, closed the schools at Athens, and procured the formal condemnation of Origen, Christian thought has been bound in the iron fetters of Augustinianism, and, in science, Aristotelean realism has reigned supreme.

But we have out-grown (or, at least, are out-growing) a scientific method which, in practice, excludes from the domain of knowledge all experience not derived through the avenues of sense, and a theology based on imperialism, and elaborated in accordance with the principles of Roman jurisprudence. Materialism has fallen into disrepute, partly because its foundations have been shaken by the phenomena of the séance room and the recognition by the faculty of hypnotism as a curative agent, and partly because it is felt to be unsatisfactory as an explanation of the Universe. And those who feel that imperialism in religion is out of harmony with that "perfect freedom" in which the service of God consists, will turn with disgust from the wretched legality of Latin theology, and welcome with joy a teacher like Origen, who claims for Christianity the distinction of the supreme philosophical system, and asserts that it is capable of being co-ordinated with all forms of human activity—physical, mental, and spiritual.

Now this is exactly what Madame Blavatsky, the founder of Modern Theosophy, claims on behalf of the religio-philosophical system which she has given to the world, and it is the foundation of its alleged superiority over all other religions, which it professes to include and interpret. In other words, she has aimed at establishing a rival Catholic Church, and those who believe that "other foundation can no man lay than that which *is* laid" will do well to examine the grounds of Theosophic belief and practice, and the pretensions of the Theosophical Society to Catholicity.

In regard to Madame Blavatsky herself, as I hope to show, there is reason for believing that she was ignorant, for the most part, of the true sources of her inspiration ; that she was an instrument in the hands of unscrupulous persons who made unfair use of her remarkable gifts and exploited her, so to speak, for purposes of their own ; and that, when more is known of the nature of the conflict which raged around her unhappy personality, she will be regarded as more sinned against than sinning. Moreover, I hope to shew that, in spite of her vast knowledge (obtained Heaven knows where, but almost certainly not from Thibet), she displays, at times, an extra-ordinary ignorance which it is difficult to account for except on the hypothesis of a deliberate intention to deceive the uninitiated. Her "Secret Doctrine," too, is exceedingly faulty, both in regard to its cosmo-genesis and its anthropogenesis, especially the latter ; and is, besides, tinctured and pervaded by her person-ality to an extent which seriously impairs its value as a scientific work. Added to which her passionate invective, her perversion of facts when they do not happen to fit in with her theories, and her sectarian animus in favour of any and every non-Christian religious system (Judaism alone excepted) all combine to render her a most unsafe guide to the Higher Wisdom.

With the history of the conflict " behind the veil," which resulted in the formation of the Theosophical Society, I have dealt in the first lecture. The question with which we are immediately concerned is what should be our attitude towards a system which, on its scientific side, is receiving almost daily confirmation, and which professes to give the answer to intellectual and moral problems which modern Christianity, by its own confession, is unable to solve ? In regard to the former, it is generally taken for granted that nothing can be known except that which is capable of being acquired by the ordinary recognised methods of research, and all statements which do not fall within that category are stigmatised as "unscientific." But this is to erect an arbitrary criterion of value wholly inadequate as a standard of measurement for certain kinds of truths. The ordinary recognised methods, though very excellent in their way, are not the only methods by which we can arrive at truth. There are others, recognised at present by comparatively few persons, which will become ordinary in due time, when the rank and file of men have evolved certain faculties of which they now possess only the rudiments.

Of such a nature are the methods by which much that is contained in these lectures that will be unfamiliar to the ordinary reader has been discovered ; and, if accepted at all, must be accepted on its own merits by that faculty of spiritual discernment which corresponds to what is called the "musical ear," whereby numerical relations are perceived between vibrations of the air which are much too rapid to leave any impression of number on the intellect. It will not be denied that, if we wish to arrive at truth, we must focus all knowledge within our grasp, let it come from whatever source or travel by whatever road it may. An illustration will make this clear. Mr. Norman Lockyer bases his theory of the meteoric origin of the Universe almost exclusively on chemical researches. If, however, the mathematician shews that the required curves could, or could not, have been fashioned by the postulated forces, no sane investigator would refuse to listen because the results were not arrived at by means of the crucible or the spectroscope.

In dealing, therefore, with such subjects as man's origin and destiny, his place in the Universe, the mysteries of life and mind, and other problems which modern science is unable to solve, we have no alternative but to rest in ignorance, or accept provisionally any information which seems likely to dispel the darkness in which they are shrouded.

On the other hand, the religious element in Theosophy has caused the dry bones of ecclesiasticism to shake. Dr. Newman is reported to have said at Rome, on the occasion of his investiture as Cardinal, that he saw "no hope for religion save in a new revelation." Would it not be as well to ascertain first whether we have neglected any old revelation? When an evil and adulterous generation sought after a sign, they were told that no sign should be given them but the sign of the Prophet Jonas, or the Resurrection. When a sceptical and materialistic generation ask for a new revelation, what wonder if they should receive a similar answer, and find it in a resurrection of ideas which they thought were long since dead and buried?

Few will deny that in the present day we have need for fuller information in regard to the immaterial Universe than the Jewish Scriptures afford, and, if so, why should we hesitate to search Hindu and other Scriptures, and endeavour to penetrate the veil of symbol and myth beneath which, it is asserted, lies the very knowledge which will enable science and religion, so long separated from each other, to join hands once more. For, strange as it may sound to modern Christians, it is a truth to which several of the early Fathers bore witness that the Gentiles were

the recipients of a revelation, different in character
from, but equally important with that given to the
Jews, and that the right of Christianity to be called
the " Catholic Faith " rests on the recognition of this
principle. Broadly speaking, the one Revelation was
of a moral, the other of an intellectual character. To
the Jews were given the Law and the Prophets ; their
revelation was mainly a rule of conduct, and had for
its object the formation of a national polity which
should serve as a model to all succeeding ages. In
the case of the Gentiles, revelation took another form.
It was of a scientific character, and had to do with
such important subjects as the origin and nature of
the cosmos, of the constitution and character of the
spiritual intelligences who preside over what are called
" natural forces," the laws by which they are governed,
and other mysterious truths. Both these revelations
were imperfect, for both were partial. The revelation
of God's righteousness, as it was gradually unfolded,
satisfied the moral nature of the chosen people in each
successive generation, but it did not concern itself
with their intellectual development. The wisdom of
the Gentiles was not for them until they had learned
thoroughly the lesson that the beginning of all true
wisdom is the fear of the Lord. On the other hand,
the moral element was of necessity excluded by the
form of the Gentile revelation. "The world by
wisdom knew not God," but it prepared them to

B

receive the fuller revelation of the Christian dispensation which is alone capable of satisfying the religious
instinct in man without, at the same time, dwarfing
or degrading our conceptions of God.

There can be little doubt that the failure of modern
Christianity to meet the intellectual requirements of
the age is largely due to the mistaken idea that the
Jewish Scriptures, in themselves, are a complete revelation, and that the gift of Divine Inspiration was
restricted to one people and to one period of the
world's history. This narrowness is entirely foreign
to the spirit of Christianity. All truth is the heritage
of the Catholic Church,* and as there can be no real
opposition between one truth and another, it is our
duty to "prove all things and hold fast that which
is good" from whatever source it comes. This was
so clearly perceived by the Greek Fathers that they
did not hesitate to claim Divine Inspiration for
the heathen philosophers. "Those who lived under
the guidance of the Eternal Reason (μετα λογου
βιώσαντες)," said Justin Martyr, "such as Socrates,
Heraclitus, etc., were Christians, even though in their
day they were called atheists."†

If, therefore, instead of denouncing Theosophy as
false and anti-Christian, we were to endeavour to ascertain how much truth it contains, whether its

---

* S. John xvi., 13.   † Apol. i., 46.

teachings are supplementary to, or subversive of, the fundamental doctrines of Christianity as set forth in the Creeds of the undivided Church, and how far they are capable of being reconciled with the great central doctrine of the Incarnation, we should display, not only a more reasonable, but a more Christian spirit. We should do well to bear in mind the advice of Origen, and in dealing with such doctrines as "Karma" and re-incarnation, "bring to the comprehension of subjects of such difficulty a perfect and instructed understanding. For if our minds be full of preconceptions and prejudices *on other points*, we may judge them (hastily) to be heretical and opposed to the faith of the Church, *yielding not so much to the convictions of reason as to the dogmatism of prejudice.*"* Origen himself, though he had probably never heard of "Karma," was of opinion that it was "more in conformity with reason to believe that every soul, for certain mysterious objects, is introduced into a body *according to its deserts and former actions*," rather than to suppose a fresh soul created for every child born into the world.†

What we have to do is to weigh the evidence for and against this or that theory of the Universe, and to accept the one which explains the greatest number of facts. In these lectures I have endeavoured, to the

* De Princip. vi., 1.   † Cont. Celsum, Book I., xxxii.

best of my ability, to apply this principle to the
revelations of which Madame Blavatsky was the
medium, and have arrived at the following conclusions.   (1) That modern Theosophy, highly in-
teresting and important as it may be from a scientific
point of view, is not adapted to ethical uses. Regarded
as a cosmogony, despite its faults, it is a valuable con-
tribution to occult science.   Every European occultist
must acknowledge that it has opened up for investigation vast tracts of hitherto unexplored territory.
As a philosophy, however, (2) it leaves much to be
desired, for it makes no attempt to solve the problem
of free-will, which is the very essence of personality.
It is too fatalistic ; while, (3) considered as a religion,
Theosophy lacks motive power, affording no materials
on which to found that altruism on which Theosophists
so strongly insist. A belief in " Karma " and re-incarnation can supply, at best, a selfish motive for doing
good, and, at its worst, paralyze all individual effort.
Altruism can never be anything but a barren dogma
when it has only an utilitarian basis.   In other words,
belief in the brotherhood of man is inseparable from
belief in the Fatherhood of God, which is denied by
the Theosophists, as inconsistent with that imper-
sonality which, they say, is essential to the conception
of a Divine Being.

But this denial is fatal to the claim of modern
Theosophy to represent the " Ancient Wisdom

Religion," for no religion that ever existed taught the absurdity of an impersonal God. Even "Positivism," that Frankenstein monster of a materialistic philosophy, professes belief in a shadowy personality which is supposed to inhere in the resultant of the sum total of human activity, and is dignified by the name of Humanity, with a capital "H." Of course the worship (if genuine) is idolatry, for "the Catholic Faith is this: that we worship One God in Trinity, and the Trinity in Unity," and the worship of any other god is idolatry, whether the "Eidolon" be "Humanity" (*i.e.*, creature worship), or a metaphysical conception of the indefinite masquerading as the Infinite, or a hideously carved block of wood.

Religion is the bond which unites man with God. It may take many forms, but only one which is adapted for all men and all times. The doctrine of the WORD MADE FLESH is alone capable, I repeat, of satisfying at once the religious instinct in man without at the same time dwarfing and degrading our conception of God.

Christianity is above all others a comprehensive religion. It proclaims One Lord, One Faith, One Baptism. Its one Lord is the Head of the human race, its one Faith is the key to all mysteries, its one Baptism is the witness to the solidarity of mankind,— that organic unity which, if recognised, would resolve into harmony all conflicting opinions about religion, which derive their vitality from conflicting interests, by establishing a direct relation with the Spirit of Truth, from Whom proceed all forms of intellectual activity.

In every age, the prevailing religious tendency is reflected in the special characteristic of its art. The enthusiastic nature worship of the ancient Greeks resulted in the idealisation of form, but their colour-sense was undeveloped. Their genius was plastic. In the middle ages, the so-called " ages of faith," the unseen cast strange lights and shadows on the world of sense, often distorting its natural forms and directing men's attention to its shifting and evanescent aspects, which it belongs to the art of the painter to fix and render permanent in beauty of colour and arrangement. But, in these days, we have lost faith in the unseen world, and science has destroyed our conceptions of nature as the mild mother, and revealed her as inexorable law. We are oppressed by her awfulness, and seek to discover some means whereby we can escape to a region where the pain and turmoil of the lower world may be ideally resolved into elements of beauty. And in music we find this ideal region. All art is symbolic, and is the expression of some spiritual reality, and music, which is emphatically the *modern* art, as painting and architecture were the arts of the middle ages and sculpture of ancient Greece, is the voice of the present age crying out against the discords of the world and seeking to resolve them into harmony. The Universe is, in truth, a grand symphony. Its theme is God's Love, and its keynote is "*Et Incarnatus est de Spiritu Sancto ex Maria Virgine.*"

We are approaching the end of an important cycle in the evolution of humanity, and in these, as in all other "last days," there is an outpouring of the Spirit of Wisdom. The words of the prophet Joel, if we interpret them aright, are as applicable to the end of the nineteenth century as to the end of the Jewish dispensation. Our sons and daughters, the intellectual offspring of the century and the parents of twentieth century thought, are beginning to prophesy. Let us not turn a deaf ear. Our young men, the most vigorous of our scientists, are beginning to see visions, and the visions of a Crookes, a Keely, or a Tesla, it would be folly to despise. And our old men, or those whose intellectual life belongs wholly to this century, and who have no inheritance in the next—our Spencers, Huxleys, "orthodox" theologians and political economists—are dreaming vain dreams ere the age sinks to sleep. But now, as then, "it shall come to pass that all who call upon the Name of the Lord shall be saved." The winds of false doctrine may shake and the waves of heresy may threaten, but can never engulf the "Faith once delivered to the Saints," for it is founded on a Rock, an Eternal Truth which is a key to every problem in the universe.

LECTURE I.

SCIENCE (or systematized knowledge) is of three kinds—physical, mental, and spiritual.

Physical science deals with external phenomena ; mental science, with the truths about relations, such as number, position and motion ; and spiritual science, with the truths of harmony—an eternal principle in Nature, to which the art of music is an endeavour to give symbolic expression through the medium of vibrations in the atmosphere having a definite numerical relation to each other.

Spiritual science is frequently called "Occult Science." The term has been much abused, chiefly on account of its connexion with certain arts, such as divination, necromancy, witchcraft, and especially modern spiritualism, which is neither an art nor a science, but a dangerous playing with edge tools. Such arts may be, and are, practised with as little knowledge of occult science as a telegraph clerk need possess of the science of electrical engineering. But there is a science founded on a knowledge, more or less perfect, of the laws which govern the spiritual region of causes, which has been handed down for centuries by oral tradition, and jealously guarded from the vulgar by an elaborate symbolism so con-

trived as to answer the double purpose of concealment from the unworthy, and suggestiveness whereby
those who have developed the faculty of spiritual
discernment up to a certain point may be stimulated
to further inquiry.

The reason for this secrecy is that the knowledge
in question is the key to a power which would be
highly dangerous to society (as at present constituted)
if it were to become public property. The spiritual
region is, as I have just said, the world of *cause.*
What are called "natural forces" have their origin
on the same plane of existence as the human will,
for between man and the Universe there is a mysterious correspondence. The foundation (or "substance," as the schoolmen called it) of matter is
force, and the spiritual force of man's individuality
being the ultimate (objective) force in nature, it can
analyse and dissolve all secondary chemical and
mechanical forces. Given a certain kind of knowledge, and it is possible to develope, by training,
powers latent in every individual which would be
so many weapons in the hands of unscrupulous persons that would enable them to commit crimes
without the least fear of detection. Such a state
of things would inaugurate a reign of terror that
would shake society to its foundations. This, indeed,
once actually happened. The traditions preserved
among all nations of a universal flood are a witness

to this catastrophe. There is a certain periodic law of cataclysms which comes into operation under such circumstances and, to a great extent, neutralises the evil, as will be explained in a succeeding lecture.

It is, however, impossible to guard the fortress of spiritual science at all points, and a breach, once made, is very easily widened, for sciences have a tendency to overlap one another. Chemistry, for example, which is a physical science, has, for some time past, received, in its higher branches, valuable aid from mathematics, or pure mental science. The discovery of the rare metal "Gallium" is a case in point. Mr. Mendeleef of St. Petersburg had predicted from a study of the atomic numbers of the elements that a metal would be found to fill a vacant place in the series, and gave its probable specific gravity, which agrees closely with the results of the experiments at Paris with Gallium.

In the same way, it is now almost past praying for that our physical scientists will continue to ignore the phenomena of the séance room and the latest developments of hypnotism. Directly these become subjects of investigation by a large number of trained observers for the purpose of ascertaining the relation they bear to the mystery of life and mind—what relation, for example, electric conditions set up by the action of the human will bear towards similar conditions in inorganic substances—it is almost impossible that certain natural forces should fail to be discovered, and the methods by which they may be manipulated, which our scientific men, in accordance with their usual custom, will immediately make public. This will constitute a serious danger, but one which it is impossible to avoid. Accordingly it has been deemed advisable by some who possess the key to the higher knowledge to impart to those who choose to receive them certain facts, until lately kept secret because they were part of a secret whole, which, until quite recently, there existed no special reason for making known.

Of the reasons for this decision, and the causes which have led up to it, I purpose now to treat.

Occultists are divided into "practical" and "theoretical." With practical occultism, or the science of "Magic," these lectures do not profess to deal. It is necessary to state, however, that there are two kinds of magic—*white* and *black*. The subject of black magic is too revolting for anything but the briefest mention. The nearest approach . in the Universe to anything like the popular conception of a devil is the Black Magician. When I say that the torture of animals is recommended as. an excellent training for developing the faculties essential to the successful practice of black magic, I shall probably give you a better idea of its nature than any actual description of its horrible rites would convey; though, in regard to these, I may say that if, *per impossibile*, I could bring myself to repeat in English the words of a certain incantation (said to be of Moorish origin though in bastard Latin) it would have the effect of clearing the room in five minutes.

White magic is the ministry of healing, not only of physical, but mental and moral disease. It must not be supposed, however, that the practical occultist is (quâ occultist) a doctor, a philosopher, or a minister of religion. He may be each and all of these, and in other ages and countries combined and monopolised the three. But his real work is on the higher plane of causes. It is very difficult to convey to the uninitiated a clear idea of the nature of an operation in white magic. It is something like a religious function— indeed, the religious functions of the Church were sometimes utilised for the purpose on the Continent, until the ecclesiastical authorities discovered and put a stop to it from jealousy and a wish to keep all spiritual power in their own hands.

The ritual of the *Higher Magic* differs, however, in several important respects from any exoteric function, and writers like *Eliphas Levi* may be searched in vain for any information in regard to the actual essentials which are never committed to writing. "Le Dogme et Rituel de la Haute Magie" is, nevertheless, a monument of learning from an historical point of view, and contains many curious details in connection with evil, or at any rate, *doubtful* operations which constitute its chief interest. At least, so I am given to understand, for I am not myself a practical occultist. I am also informed that of late years the ritual has been much simplified. The dramatic element (if I may use the expression), which at one time had its use, has almost disappeared, and with it all the paraphernalia of robes, crossed swords, and barren verbiage. The place of the swords has been taken by pointed copper rods, which are found to answer the purpose better, while Turkish Baths and Jaeger Clothing are amply sufficient for all purposes of cleanliness.

But ceremonial magic is only practised by certain orders, and resorted to in exceptional circumstances. It is attended with considerable danger to the intellect, and in all White Brotherhoods is discouraged, and in some forbidden under pain of expulsion, for the reason that it exposes to a peculiar form of temptation, viz., to suicide.

A practical occultist usually belongs to a brotherhood, and I am given to understand that many of them are members of the higher orders of Freemasons, and constitute in that body an *imperium in imperio*. Others there are who belong to religious orders in the Roman Catholic Church, notably the *Jesuits*, to which

they stand in the same relation as the others to the
Freemasons. Between these and the last named there
is war to the knife, and each accuses the other of
following the " left-hand path."   There are, of course,
exceptions to this rule ; I know myself one practical
occultist who is unattached, but the advantages of
co-operation are so great that nearly every *practical*
occultist (unless he has given himself up to the practice
of evil arts) is a member of some one or other more
or less strict fraternity. A theoretical occultist, on the
other hand, is not necessarily a member of an esoteric
brotherhood, though, of course, many of them are.
There are numbers of self-initiated persons in this
country, for various reasons precluded from taking
the steps necessary to attain proficiency in practical
occultism, who are yet in intimate relation with those
who have, and whose companionship, and even advice,
are sought and welcomed by those who are taking an
active part in the combat behind the veil.

Occultists (both practical and theoretical) may be
divided into three parties.   " Esoterics," Liberals, and
Brothers of the "Left."   In one sense, of course, every
occultist is an " Esoteric " in the same way that every
politician, however advanced (provided he stops short
of actual Nihilism), is a Conservative.

No one who has passed the " Dweller on the
Threshold " could ever be tempted to reveal the secret
of the Threshold, for only a madman would saw off

the branch on which he sits. It is the knowledge that pertains to the region beyond about which there are differences of opinion as to how much it is prudent to reveal. Much of this knowledge it would be a plain duty to communicate to the world, if we were sure it would not be misused. Certain facts connected with human generation it would be useful for everyone to know. Many of the evils which spring from ignorance of the causes of disease might be easily averted, and the diseases themselves removed without recourse to drugs. Much time and labour might be saved if the ratio of consonant etheric vibrations were known, and our skilful mechanicians thus in a position to avail themselves of "nature's finer forces."

But the trouble is that none of these things could be revealed by themselves. The mystery of birth and death is a key to the portals of an unseen world inhabited by man's most deadly foes ; deadly on account of the sympathy which exists between his lower and their higher nature, constituting a fatal bond of attraction wholly evil in its effects on humanity.

In the same way, the knowledge of how to cure disease cannot be separated from the knowledge of how to produce it, and it is a very grave question whether, on the whole, the diffusion of this knowledge would be a blessing or a curse as society is at present constituted.

And the same argument applies with enormous force to placing in the hands of the rich a power which would enable them to dispense with nine-tenths of the labour which at present ministers to their wants, and, at the same time, provide them with the means of instantly crushing any hostile demonstation on the part of the unemployed majority, who would then be entirely at their mercy. Such a power in the hands of a few individuals would inaugurate a state of things too appalling to contemplate.

Ex tribus, disce omnes. The party of secrecy among occultists has a very strong case. It is not from pride, or the love of mystery for its own sake, far less is it from mere churlish selfishness, that they hold the key of knowledge with so tenacious a grasp. I am not an "Esoteric" myself; otherwise I should not deliver these lectures, but though I yield to none as to the importance of discretion, I am unable to agree with many persons whom I hold in the highest respect as to the wisdom of continuing the policy of total silence, until lately preserved, in regard to the very existence in these days of such a science as occultism, and what I cannot help calling the Jesuitical practice of siding with the Philistines against "mediæval superstitions" in the public press. Being "*unattached*," I consider myself at liberty to express my opinion freely on this point.

There is, however, what may be called a liberal

party among occultists, and like the liberal party in politics, it is accused by the conservatives of departing from the principles of the liberals of a generation ago. Liberalism has been defined as "*trust in the people tempered with discretion*," and its opposite "*mistrust of the people tempered by fear*." The definition is, on the whole, a sound one, and if the political liberals of the last generation would now be called conservatives, the "liberal" occultists of fifty years ago were certainly "esoterics" so far as the policy of total secrecy was concerned. But the times were different. The gross materialism of the first half of the nineteenth century had to be destroyed before any instruction could be conveyed. Accordingly, the efforts of the liberals of the last generation were concentrated on the indirect production of the phenomena known as modern Spiritualism. The agitation for the Repeal of the Corn Laws which took place in the political world about the same time, was not more hotly conducted than the conflict "behind the veil" on the question of Spiritualism. Those who were in favour of this experiment on modern habits of thought were denounced as Brothers of the Left, and even Black Magicians; in the same way that Bright and Cobden were reviled as levellers, atheists, and enemies of society generally. I regret to say that the results in the political and the occult world have not been the same. The Esoterics have triumphed, and the Psychical Research

C

Society are bewailing the dearth of "phenomena" and the rarity of "genuine" mediums.

There is yet a third party among occultists, who are called by their opponents "Brothers of the Left" (*i.e.,* the left-hand path), and sometimes "Brothers of the Shadow," which last name has given rise to the curious mistake of confounding them with Black Magicians. The true Black Magician is almost unknown in Europe, though the practice of evil arts is, I regret to say, far from uncommon, especially by amateurs. But the Black Magician is an Ishmael among occultists. His hand is against every man, and every man's hand against him. There are no "Black" brotherhoods, for there can be no mutual confidence between men who are wholly self-centred.

A "Brother of the Shadow" is something quite different from the individual with the red fillet in Mrs. Campbell Praed's shilling shocker. The Shadow has nothing to do with shady morals. It is, to speak plainly, the Papacy—the Shadow, or "ghost" as Gibbon calls it, of the Old Roman Empire. Under its baleful influence the sense of individual responsibility withers. Right and wrong become synonymous with obedience and disobedience to the spiritual authority ; and among the Jesuits, we have the sad spectacle of the highest knowledge and the noblest powers perverted into instruments for obtaining an unfair advantage in the conduct of political intrigues (often in them-

selves of a very questionable character) which have for
their object the re-establishment of the temporal
power of the Pope. I do not doubt for a moment that
they are honest in their belief that this is necessary for
the spiritual welfare of Europe, but the doctrine that
"the end justifies the means" is a doctrine of the
Shadow, not of the Light.

But of course all Brothers of the Left are not Jesuits,
though these are the most powerful and important.
Without entering into further details, suffice it to say
that the term is used to designate *practical* occultists
who devote their energies to the promotion of objects
which have for their aim the interests of the few
rather than the good of humanity in general. I shall
have occasion to refer to them again in connection
with the Theosophical movement.

For the present I wish to say a few words in
connection with the phenomena of the Séance room—
what is known as Modern Spiritualism. It has an
unfortunate history.

About the year 1840 the nations of modern Europe
touched a certain point in their evolutionary cycle
called the "*point of physical intellectuality.*" One of
those crises had arrived which necessitated immediate
action of *some* kind on the part of those who keep
watch over the signs of the times. For, in the life of
nations, there is a periodic ebb and flow of tendency—
alternate periods of intellectual and spiritual evolution

of varying strength. This variation is subject to a
law of increase and diminution in a constant ratio for
each, which I will endeavour to explain in a future
lecture. At the period of which I am speaking, the
spiritual evolution was proceeding at its minimum, and
the intellectual at its maximum rate, and a strong
current had set in towards Materialism in all departments of human activity. Now the great danger of
Materialism is the adoption of an utilitarian standard
of goodness ; and intellectual *evolution*, under these
conditions, is spiritual *involution*, or death.

It became, therefore, a serious question with occultists
(1) how far they were justified in concealing longer the
fact that there is an unseen world around us as real
as the world of sense, and (2) how this could be
revealed with safety. In other words, how could a
safe course be steered between Scylla and Charybdis.

It was admitted on all hands that something must
be done, but the party of secrecy were averse to a
straightforward policy of tentative elementary instruction. " Let us proceed cautiously " they said in effect,
" and endeavour to ascertain indirectly how far the
public is disposed to receive such instruction." Accordingly experiments were made, first in America, then in
France, and afterwards in England, with certain
individuals of a peculiar psychical organisation, since
called mediums. But the whole thing was a failure.
The mediums, one and all, declared that they were

controlled by spirits who had departed from the earth.
" It was just what might have been expected,". said
those who are always wise after the event, but, in point
of fact, no one had expected it. I can only account
for this strange oversight by the fact that " the children
of this world are wiser in their generation than the
children of light." The occultists were like the man
in the fable who was so absorbed in the contemplation
of the stars that he walked into the ditch at his feet.

As, under the circumstances, the " Spiritualists "
could not be undeceived as to the source of their
inspirations, there was no alternative but to with-
draw from the experiment. But the mischief was
done. The door had been opened to extra mundane
influences, and could not be reclosed. Spiritualism
was a Frankenstein monster, and a Proteus into
the bargain. Mediumship (especially in America)
became a profession, and mediums, subject to every
kind of psychic influence, were largely exploited by
" Brothers of the Left" for their own purposes. The
party of secrecy were almost wholly employed in
endeavouring to counteract these influences with
the assistance of many who called themselves
" Liberals " (quite a new name by the way) when
an event occurred which united both parties in
defence against a common danger. A person who
was known to exist, but who had not been discovered, suddenly appeared in Paris, presented her-

self at an occult lodge, and demanded admission into the brotherhood on terms which could not be entertained for a moment. She then disappeared, and the next thing that was heard was that a certain Madame Blavatsky had been expelled from an American brotherhood for an offence against the constitution of the United States,* and had gone to British India in order to carry out a certain threat which it would seem there was a fair prospect of her putting into execution.

It is only within the last few months† that I learned the details of this Homeric struggle in which poor Madame Blavatsky played the part of Patroclus in the armour of Achilles. Like Patroclus, she spread consternation at first, but was soon (metaphorically) slain, or rather, taken prisoner. Then it was that the real battle began, and for several years raged around her unhappy personality. But as I am not at liberty to make unrestricted use of the information I received, the best way will be to read an extract from a report which I drew up at the time with the view (since abandoned) of putting it in the hands of the newspaper readers in the form of an

---

* This is a most extraordinary statement. I will not vouch for its truth and cannot even hazard a guess as to the nature of the offence. Indeed it raises a suspicion that the American fraternity was a brotherhood of the "Left," especially when taken in conjunction with what follows.

† 1893.

interview. In order to make it more easily comprehended I used political terms, such as "Liberal," "Conservative," "Coalition Ministry," etc., which, I need hardly say, must only be taken in a figurative sense. The first part, it will be observed, covers ground we have already traversed.

Our conversation having turned on the Theosophical movement in Europe and America, I gathered the following information :—

(1) That the phenomena of the séance room are not due to the spirits of the dead, but of the living ; that modern spiritualism is an experiment on modern civilization decided on, about fifty years ago, by a federation of occult brother- . hoods for the purpose of testing its vitality and ascertaining whether it is capable of receiving new truths without danger.

(2) That there are what may be called a "Liberal" and "Conservative" party amongst occultists, and that the rank and file are strongly Conservative, though about two-thirds of the leaders are more or less inclined to Liberalism ; and that, owing to the preponderance of Conservative opinion, "spiritualism" is about to receive a severe blow which will have the effect of throwing discredit on "phenomena" generally.*

---

* It does not seem to have come yet. 1894.

(3) That the "aspect of the heavens" at the time of the birth of Madame Blavatsky frightened the Conservatives," and resulted in a kind of "coalition ministry," which gave place to a Liberal one in the year 1841.

(4) That a "Brother of the Left" revealed this fact to Madame Blavatsky in Egypt about twenty years ago, that she returned to Europe immediately, and imposed certain terms as a condition of reception into an occult brotherhood in Paris, which were indignantly refused ; that she was subsequently received in America and expelled very shortly afterwards.

(5) That in consequence of a threat from Madame Blavatsky that she would soon make the American brotherhood "shut up shop," a conference of American and European occultists was held at Vienna, and a particular course of action decided upon.

(6) That during the time Madame Blavatsky imagined herself to be in Thibet, she was, in reality, at Khatmandhu in the state known to occultists as "in prison."

(7) That certain Hindu occultists who, for patriotic reasons, having sided with her against the American brotherhood, had nearly succeeded in procuring her release from "prison" by their own efforts, consented to a compromise whereby she

was to be set free on condition of their non-interference with anything that had been already accomplished. (Mr. ——— was very severe in his condemnation of these Hindu occultists who preferred the interests of their country to the interests of humanity.)

(8) That Koot Hoomi is a real person, but is neither a Thibetan nor a "Mahatma." "He is," said Mr. ———, "a treacherous scoundrel in the pay of the Russian Government, who, for a time, succeeded in deceiving Madame Blavatsky, but whose true character and personality she at length discovered." Her chagrin at having been so long hoodwinked caused her a serious illness. But as the "Mahatmas" were the foundation stone of the Theosophical Society she was obliged to keep up the deception. She contrived, however, to let "Koot Hoomi" gradually disappear as the author of "phenomena," and substituted for him a mythical "Mahatma M. ———," who never appeared in his "astral body."

(9) That it was the "Kiddle incident" which first opened her eyes to the trick which had been played on her.

(10) That it was "Koot Hoomi" who subsequently tampered with the Coulombs at Adyar—in revenge, it is supposed, at the defeat of his machinations.

(11) That, incredible as it may seem, she allowed
     herself to be again deceived after her return to
     England ; this time by a renegade Jew, who had
     been expelled from a continental brotherhood
     for the practice of evil arts.   It was decided not
     to warn her against this individual, because he
     was keeping her alive.   In her wretched state of
     health, the withdrawal of the stimulus of his
     control would have been fatal.   The man waited
     until she had completed the second volume of
     her "Secret Doctrine" and then threw her over.
     She succumbed to her next attack and died in
     1891, unsuspicious (so far as is known) to the
     last, and serenely unconscious that she had been
     all her life a tool in the hands of designing
     persons, very few of whom were her intellectual
     equals, and who made disgraceful use of her
     extraordinary mental activity and unique gifts.

Now I think it will be admitted that this throws
considerable light on a subject hitherto shrouded in
mystery.   It vindicates Madame Blavatsky from the
charge of vulgar imposture, while, at the same time,
it effectually disposes of the "Mahatma" theory.
As for the so-called miracles with the performance of
which she is credited, I see no reason to doubt that
some of them were genuine exhibitions of occult
power, or to deny that others were fraudulent.   Nor
do I attach very much importance to the moral aspect

of the latter. Those who have had any experience of the higher phenomena of Spiritualism know how difficult it is to apportion justly the blame which attaches itself equally to medium and control in cases of fraud.

For I think that there can be no doubt that Madame Blavatsky was a *medium* of a very exceptional kind. Her psychic personality was in many respects unique. Early in life she was gifted with the faculty known in Scotland as second-sight. Persons of this kind are usually " *negative* ; " that is to · say, they have seldom any strongly marked individual characteristics. But this extraordinary woman united with the utmost receptivity, a remarkable courage and independence of character. Regardless of the world's opinion, good or bad, she brushed aside social conventions as if they were so many cobwebs. She possessed a vigorous intellect, though not a *great* one, for she was deficient in the logical faculty. But her capacity for assimilating knowledge was enormous, and, I am afraid I must add, the facility with which she was capable of perverting it to suit her own ends. Like a certain famous statesman who is said to follow his conscience as a coachman follows his horses, viz., by driving them before him, so Madame Blavatsky followed truth by applying to what *is* the lash of what she considered *ought to be*. Withal she was of a most kindly disposition and impulsive generosity, and, though destitute of every distinctive feminine quality, possessed the remarkable gift of fascinating all with whom she came in contact.

Now, though I am treading on thin ice, I must add a few words in partial explanation of the mysterious phrase " in prison." What is occult " imprisonment," and why was it inflicted on Madame Blavatsky?

There is a certain operation of ceremonial magic by means of which a wall of psychic influences may be built up around an individual who has become dangerous, which has the effect of paralyzing the higher activities, and producing what is called the " repercussion of effort," and the result is a kind of spiritual sleep characterised by fantastic visions. It is an operation seldom resorted to even by Brothers of the Left, and in the case of Madame Blavatsky *was disapproved of by almost all European occultists.* On the American brotherhood alone rests the responsibility for what has since happened. The late Mr. Oliphant, I believe, knew more about the affair than any Englishman.

However, to cut a long story short, Madame Blavatsky emerged from " prison " a Thibetan Buddhist and the prophetess of a new religion.

The re-appearance of Madame Blavatsky has necessitated a total change of the policy of secrecy hitherto pursued. Whether for good or evil, she has made public an immense mass of information in regard to matters which, until quite recently, were never spoken of outside certain societies, but which is of such a character as to commend itself on its own merits to thoughtful persons from whatever source it may come. For it is the greatest mistake in the world to suppose that Theosophy depends on the evidence for the genuineness of Madame Blavatsky's "miracles" or the existence of "Mahatmas."

Indeed, since the death of Madame Blavatsky in 1891, the policy of the leading Theosophists has been to keep the "Mahatmas" as much as possible in the background. Mrs. Besant, e.g. (who, with far less knowledge than her teacher, possesses over her the great, advantage of being able to arrange her thoughts methodically) perceives quite clearly that Theosophy, if it is to succeed, must take possession of the reason and conscience of the nineteenth century. To this end she has devoted herself to expounding its doctrines with special reference to their points of contact with orthodox science, and to, intellectual and moral problems which modern Christianity has found itself unable to solve in the absence of this kind of knowledge, which is supposed to be the peculiar property of Thibetan Adepts.

Now, that Madame Blavatsky obtained her vast knowledge in the ordinary way of study is out of the question. I believe she spoke the truth when she said it was imparted to her by extraordinary methods.

She was, in fact, the medium in the hands of some person or persons unknown, who, for reasons of their own, have chosen to shelter themselves behind her personality. It really matters very little where she got her almost encyclopædic information. What we have to do is to examine it carefully in the light of knowledge we already possess. For it cannot be denied that while " Isis Unveiled " contains little that was not known before, the " Secret Doctrine " affords most valuable information in regard to pre-historic civilizations and religions, and hints at certain secrets the very existence of which was unsuspected ; some of which have been tested by a process known to occultists and found correct. And though, perhaps, outside the Theosophical Society, not one in a thousand reads the " Secret Doctrine," or one in ten thousand is capable of sifting the wheat from the chaff, it will receive more and more attention as religious thought gradually emancipates itself from Latin influences, and modern scientific discovery from atomic illusions.

LECTURE II.

AN Initiate meant originally one to whom had been imparted instructions which enabled him to penetrate the region of super-physical concepts which is hidden by a thin veil from the world of sense, and to distinguish between illusions and realities which, on the border land, are in close juxta-position to each other, and are, for this reason, a source of danger to the intellect ; for to be incapable of distinguishing illusion from reality is to become insane.

In ancient times, there was no general diffusion of knowledge by means of literature. Even in Greece, literature played a very unimportant part in education, and was confined to poetry and history. Instruction in science was oral. When committed to writing it was always veiled in symbol, and the only exoteric science was mathematics. In Egypt, Chaldea and India there could be no conflict between science and religion, for their custodians belonged to the same class or caste. However repugnant to our modern notions of equality distinctions of caste may seem, they contributed powerfully to the stability of those ancient civilizations which were in many respects far higher than our own.

But in these days, it is neither possible nor desirable

to confine knowledge to a class, except a certain kind
of knowledge ; and this is (so to speak) held in trust
for the benefit of all, and will be revealed when the
times are ripe for imparting it to the world.

Formerly, every Initiate was a member of an occult
fraternity, who had gone through a regular course of
instruction and discipline.   But, in modern times,
there are exceptions to this rule.   Facilities are
afforded, in the present day, for self-initiation, which,
in old times, did not exist, and the esoteric fraternities
have been compelled to recognise this fact and modify
their rules of secrecy accordingly.   By a very ancient
rule, every initiate can claim to be instructed by a
more learned brother, when occasion arises for action,
on points where ignorance might prove a disadvantage
to him, and I am glad to take this opportunity of
testifying to the very generous way in which such
appeals have been responded to in my own case.

What, then, is an Initiate in modern times, as
distinguished from the individual tried, proved and
admitted to instruction in the higher mysteries, which
the term formerly connoted ?

An Initiate is one who has crossed the threshold of
the unseen, with or without help ; has passed the
" Dweller," resisted the temptation to remain with her,
and, undeterred by that fear which the unknown
always inspires, has made acquaintance with the
region beyond, and reduced into order a set of

experiences, as wholly unfamiliar as is the world of sense to the new-born infant, by the ordinary common-sense process of intellectual classification.

An Initiate is *not* necessarily an Adept. He may understand the relations between the seen and the unseen world, he may have threaded the network (if I may use the expression) of causes in the unseen which unfold themselves as effects in the world of phenomena, and yet be totally unable to *control* those effects, and would shrink with dismay from the respon-sibility of taking part in a strife the preparation for which requires years of training. Who, because he has learned to handle a pair of sculls on the Serpentine, would volunteer for life-boat service in a storm at sea? or, because he has witnessed the amputation of a limb by a skilful surgeon, should consider himself qualified to perform a similar operation, and resolve to handle the knife at the first convenient opportunity?

Again, an Initiate (or an Adept either, for that matter, unless he belongs to a certain class) is not necessarily a clairvoyant. A man may be able to read even though his sight be weak, while the strongest eyes are useless to him who has not learned to read, or to whom the language is unknown. The mental sight of some Adepts is actually weak (for Adeptship is seldom attained without some loss of intellectual vigour), and they prefer to be read to, if I may be allowed the expression. To the uninitiated

D

this may seem very fanciful and extravagant, but it is a fact that, among occultists, the really great intellects are content to serve and obey, and rarely aspire to become rulers and arbiters, and this is especially the case with the astrological orders who, from time to time, give the results of their observations, but advice, never, or on very rare occasions—perhaps once or twice in a century.

Once more. An Initiate is a man who has learned a great secret which is of the nature of a paradox. It is dangerous to divine, but it is destruction to reveal. To impart it to the world would be madness, for it would have the effect of dividing humanity into Cains and Abels. To reveal it to an individual would be to put one's-self in his power for life. It is the one secret that torture is powerless to extract, for in such circumstances, the agony of revealing it under compulsion would put an end to the victim's reason and probably his life.

Now as these lectures are for the purpose of giving information and not tantalizing or mystifying, I will do my best to try and explain by analogy the nature of the strange experience to which I have referred.

The most grotesque notions prevail concerning the "Dweller on the Threshold," which probably have arisen from a too literal interpretation of the experiences of Glyndon in that magnificent allegory of "*Zanoni*," or rather let me say (since the author

disclaims the term allegory on the ground that the
characters are not personifications of abstract things
such as Virtues or Qualities) that magnificent Parable
of Human Aspirations after the Ideal. He admits,
however, that " beneath the narrative it relates, typical
meanings are concealed." He certainly did not mean
that a veiled figure, whose eyes gleam with demoniac
fire, appears to the actual sight, whether normal or
clairvoyant. In the case of Glyndon, it was the fiend
of his own unholy desires which, in the light that
flashed upon him, at the instant of crossing the threshold, appalled him by revealing, in all its native hideous-
ness, the close affinity which existed between the forces
born of the corruption of his own lower nature and the
destructive forces of the planet, constituting a fatal
bond of attraction between himself and the evil ministers of disease and death. And then came the temptation which, in the words of Zanoni, " it is forbidden
the lips to repeat, the hand to record." It can, however, be illustrated by analogy. It is easy to cross
the floor of a room between two parallel chalk lines
six inches apart. It requires great courage and steadi-
ness of nerve to cross a precipice on a six inch plank.
The temptation to step off seems almost irresistible,
and is described by those who have performed the
feat as an instinctive effort to counteract the tendency
to sway from side to side, which is the natural effect
of rapid focussing and re-focussing of the eye oppressed

by the distant detail beneath. In the same way, the difficulty of distinguishing between illusion and reality, on the border land of the unseen, tends to destroy the mental balance. The perception of hostile influences (whose nature is only revealed in the world of sense by their effects) in all their naked actuality has, for him whose lower nature is unpurified by discipline, an awful fascination. As a drowning man, the instant before unconsciousness, sees the whole of his former life, as in a rapid panorama, pass before him, so, to him who is crossing the threshold, every evil thought of which he is capable, whether translated into action or not, seems a cord grasped by hands eager to drag him into the abyss. There are no such cords, but the situation is one of intolerable horror when experienced for the first time. Presence of mind, however, is all that is required. Forewarned is forearmed, and the Dweller on the Threshold may be safely defied by him who nerves himself to disregard *physical* dangers which he *perceives* for the first time, but to which a moment's calm reflection will enable him to see that he has always been subject without knowing it, and that the knowledge itself is no danger if he will only keep cool. But to lose one's head is to court destruction. Better to die of *delirium tremens* than come under the influence of the thousand and one illusory phantoms which beset the backward path into the world of sense. I was once persuaded by a young man whose moral courage I thought could be relied upon, to impart certain instructions which, if followed out, would have enabled him to cross the threshold with safety. My last words to him as I shook hands with him at the railway station were, "Don't lose confidence in yourself, and bring your common-sense to bear in distinguishing illusions from realities." I heard from him a few weeks afterwards. At his very first supersensual experience, he dropped the whole thing like a red-hot coal, with the usual consequences—ridiculous phantasms, voices, apparitions, and what not. I wrote advising him to experiment no further, and resolving in my own mind never to take such a responsibility on myself again. Let those who wish to be instructed apply in the proper quarters. If they are in earnest, they will find out probably " quite by accident."

In concluding this part of my subject, I hope I have made it clear that the Initiate is not necessarily a magician, a clairvoyant, a prophet, or even a teacher, for he may lack the ability to co-relate accurately the laws which govern the spiritual region with those by which purely physical phenomena are regulated. But he knows the secret of the magician's power ; what the clairvoyant *sees* he is able to *read ;* and if he will take the trouble to work out certain problems, the data of which are furnished by his own actual experience, e can ascertain, after a little preliminary instruction in numerical symbolism, the relations which every visible effect bears to its invisible cause, and by applying to it the key of the " Three Great Axioms," trace its unfoldment in time with unerring accuracy.

THE THREE GREAT AXIOMS :—

I.—SEVEN IS THE PERFECT NUMBER.

II.—THE MICROCOSM IS A COPY OF THE MAC-
ROCOSM.

III.—ALL PHENOMENA HAVE THEIR ORIGIN IN
VORTICES.

These "Three Axioms" are the foundation of occult science, and are of the nature of universal truths, though not axiomatic (or self-evident) to the uninitiated, with the possible exception of No. 2, just as Axiom IX. of Euclid, " the whole is greater than its part," is as self-evident to the unreasoning dog, in the case of a biscuit, as to the reasoning man. I am not, however, concerned in defending their axiomatic character, but, on the contrary, propose to treat them as mere assertions, and inquire what can be said in favour of their probability.

Is seven the perfect number? Now the whole tendency of modern thought is to recur to the archaic idea of a homogeneous basis for apparently widely different things ; heterogeneity developed from homo-geneity, as in the search for " protoplasm " in biology; " protyle " (the name given by Mr. Crookes to the hypothetical homogeneous substance of which the atom is composed) in chemistry, and the force of which heat, electricity, light and magnetism are the differentiations.   The direction which modern science is taking is towards a generalization founded on the perception of a harmony of numbers throughout nature. So far back as the year 1844, an article appeared in the *Medical Review* in which the writer asserts the principle of a "generalization which shall express the fundamental laws of all (sciences) by *one simple numerical ratio*," and goes on to say that "from these (Whewell's 'Philosophy of the Inductive Sciences' and Mr. Hay's researches into the laws of harmonious colouring and form) it would appear that *the number seven* is distinguished in the laws regulating the harmonious perception of forms, colours and sounds, and probably of taste also if we could analyse our sensations of this kind with mathematical accuracy."*

Again, there is a periodical septenary return of cycles in the rise and fall of diseases, and in the birth, growth, maturity, decay and death of insects, reptiles, fishes, birds, mammals and man himself. Dr. Laycock (*Lancet*, 1842—3), writing on the periodicity of vita phenomena records "a most remarkable illustration and confirmation of the law in insects," and having

---

* *Medical Review*, July, 1844.—Quoted from *Secret Doctrine*.

given a number of illustrations from natural history, he adds, "The facts I have briefly glanced at are general facts and cannot happen day after day in so many millions of animals of every kind, *from the larva or ovum of a minute insect up to man*, at definite periods, from a mere chance or concidence. . . . . I think it is impossible to come to any less general conclusion than this : that, in animals, changes occur in every three-and-a-half, seven, fourteen, twenty-one or twenty-eight days, or at some definite number of *weeks*." In regard to fevers, the same Dr. Laycock states that "whatever type the fever may exhibit, there will be a paroxysm on the *seventh* day . . . . the fourteenth will be remarkable as a day of amendment," either cure or death taking place. "If the fourth (paroxysm) be severe, and the fifth less so, the disease will end at the *seventh* paroxysm, and . . . . change for the better will be seen on the *fourteenth* day, namely about three or four o'clock a.m., when the system is most languid." "This law," he says elsewhere, "binds all periodic vital phenomena together, and links the periods observed in the lowest annulose animals with those of man himself, the highest of the vertebrata."

Now if the mysterious Septenary Cycle be a law in nature ; if it is found controlling the evolution and involution (or death) in the realms of entomology, ichthyology and ornithology, as in the kingdom of the animal, mammalia and man, why cannot it be present and active in the Kosmos in general, and why should not an occultist be able to trace the same law in the life of the solar system, the planet and the races of men which inhabit it ? The number Seven is the factor element in occult science and in every ancient religion, because it is the factor element in nature.*

And this brings us to the second axiom, "The microcosm is a copy of the macrocosm." This is the law of correspondence which is the foundation of the true occult science (or rather art) of divination by number, and is dependent on the septenary constitution of the universe. Every series of which seven is the numerical ratio is a "cosmos" in itself, and is *relatively* great or small. The highest expression of this law is the individual man who is the Microcosm *par excellence*. Shakespeare's "Seven Ages of Man" is, of course, purely fanciful. From birth to death there are only five periods : infancy, childhood, youth, maturity and decline. Infancy, however, is preceded by a gestation period ending at birth, and decline is succeeded by a corresponding period of unconscious earth life, which begins with the death of the body, and ends with a return of consciousness under totally different conditions. The corresponding macrocosm is the life of the *nation*, which, in its turn, is the microcosm of the macrocosmic *race*.

"The Secret Doctrine."—Vol. ii., 623.

Putting aside the two unconscious periods with which, for our present purpose, it is not necessary to deal, but which, nevertheless, have their analogues in nation and race, we find the same phenomena of birth, growth and death repeated on a larger scale in the national life, as distinguished from that of the individuals of which the nation is compound.

Let us take modern Europe as an illustration. With the exception of the Sclavonic peoples, of whom we shall speak presently, and a small Turanian element which is too insignificant to deal with, the nations of modern Europe and their American and colonial off-shoots, represent the fifth sub-race of the great Aryan root-race. In the days of the Roman Empire, these nations were in their infancy. Before the Roman conquest, Gaul, Britain and Germany were not nations, they had only a tribal existence. Their conquest and incorporation into the Roman Empire marked the period of infancy. Roman law was their nurse and protector. To the nurse, succeeded the tutor. The destruction of the Roman Empire and the rise of the Papacy marked the period of childhood, or the beginning of their intellectual life. The period of youth, with its wider interests and enlarged range of vision, began with the Renaissance and ended with the Reformation. The manhood of modern Europe dates from the sixteenth century. We might pursue the analogy further, but the next

period, the French Revolution, brings us too close to
modern times to render it advisable at the present
stage of our inquiries to dogmatise in regard to its
significance. Let us turn to the Sclavonic people
who belong to the *sixth* Aryan sub-race, and what do
we find ? A powerful empire which unites under a
despotic government a number of local communes—
Russia. The remains of a kingdom—Poland, whose
only cohesive force is its religion, and which will be
ultimately re-absorbed in the Russian Empire in spite
of it. A number of tribes who, oppressed by the
alien Turk, have thrown off the yoke, and have been
artificially consolidated into little states, whose independence will last as long as, and no longer, than the
next great European war. What are all these but the
characteristics of a sub-race in its infancy ? Western
Europeans are accustomed to speak of its barbarism,
and in one sense they are right. Our civilization is a
mere veneer on the upper classes, and is as much
a foreign growth as Roman civilization in Britain.
Their destiny is to evolve a higher civilization of their
own in the future. The Russian Empire must die that
the Russian people may live, and the realization of
the dreams of the Pan-slavists will indicate that the
sixth Aryan sub-race has begun to live its own
intellectual life, and is no longer in its period of
infancy. We need not pursue the subject further
than to say that the national character will enable

them to carry out experiments in Socialism, political and economical, which would present innumerable difficulties in Western Europe. The above are only given as illustrations of a law which is of universal application, and is known in occult science as the "law of correspondence." It must be borne in mind that, in occult science, the *deductive* method is pursued for purposes of discovery, and the *inductive* for proof.

We come now to the third axiom, "All phenomena are the result of vortical action." What light can modern science throw on this? I have already referred to the tendency of modern science to seek for a homogeneous principle in nature, and to this hypothetical entity Mr. Crookes has given the name of *protyle*. Protyle is, so to speak, the stuff of which atoms are composed. Now, what is this "protyle"— is it force or is it matter? If "protyle" be matter, it must be divisible, and to admit the divisibility of the atom is equivalent to an admission of the infinite divisibility of matter, which materialists are compelled to deny. Büchner, for example, says that "to accept infinite divisibility is absurd, and amounts to doubting the very existence of matter." The atom then is indivisible. But, as Professor Butlerof points out (Scientific letters), it is also *elastic*. "An attempt to deprive it of elasticity is unthinkable, and would amount to an absurdity. Absolutely non-elastic atoms could never exhibit a single one of those numerous phenomena that are attributed to their correlations. Without any elasticity the atoms could not manifest their energy, and the *substance* of the materialists would remain weeded of every force. Therefore, if the Universe is composed of atoms, those atoms *must be elastic.* It is here that we meet with an insuperable obstacle. For what are the conditions required for the manifestation of elasticity? An elastic ball when striking against an obstacle is flattened and contracts, which would be impossible were it not to consist of *particles*, the relative position of which experiences, at the time of the blow, a temporary change. . . . In other words elasticity can pertain only to those bodies that are divisible and the *atom is elastic.*"

"Protyle" then is not matter, but is it force? Let us quote Professor Butlerof again, " What is Force from a strictly scientific standpoint, and as warranted by the laws of the conservation of energy? Conceptions of force arise from our conceptions of this, that, or another mode of motion." It is the translation of one state of motion into another state of the same. But motion implies a something moved, and this something, as we have seen, cannot be matter, for the infinite divisibility of atoms precludes the possibility of conceiving matter as an objective reality. Protyle, or the homogeneous basis of atoms, is, therefore, motion in an unknown medium, or *pure objective force,* and atoms are simple force centres. Is their motion vortical? Such at least is Professor Crookes' opinion. In an address delivered at Birmingham before the Chemical Section of the British Association he calls attention to the existence of bodies "which, though neither compounds or mixtures, are not *elements* in the strictest sense of the word—bodies which I venture to call 'meta-elements.'" After giving a large number of examples of bodies, apparently the same, which, yet, when examined very closely, were found to exhibit differences which, however imperceptible, still shew that none of them are simple bodies, Mr. Crookes is obliged to find some means of reconciling the new discovery with the old "periodic theory" which stands in the way of an unlimited multiplication of elements.

"That theory," he says, "has received such abundant verification that we cannot lightly accept any interpetation of phenomena which fails to be in accordance with it. But if we suppose the elements reinforced by a vast number of bodies, slightly differing from each other in their properties, and forming, if I may use the expression, aggregations of nebulæ where we formerly saw, or believed we saw, separate stars, the periodic arrangement can no longer be definitely grasped. *No longer, that is, if we retain our usual conception*

of an element. Let us then modify this conception.   For element, let us read ' elementary
group'—such elementary groups taking the place
of the old elements in the periodic scheme—and
the difficulty falls away.   In defining an element,
let us take, not an external boundary, but an
internal type.   Let us say, *e.g.*, the smallest pon-
derable quantity of yttrium is an assemblage of
ultimate atoms almost infinitely more like each
other than they are to the atoms of any approxi-
mating element.   It does not necessarily follow
that the atoms shall be all absolutely alike among
themselves.   The atomic weight which we as-
cribed to yttrium, therefore, merely represents a
mean value around which the actual weights of
the individual atoms of the 'element' range within
certain limits.   But if my conjecture is tenable,
could we separate atom from atom, we should
find them varying within narrow limits on each
side of the mean.   The very process of fractiona-
tion implies the existence of such differences in
certain bodies."

He goes on to say that " this deviation from absolute
homogeneity . . . will perhaps be clearer if we
return in imagination to the earliest dawn of our
material universe, and, face to face with the great
secret, try to consider the processes of elemental
evolution." The result at which he arrives is, as far as

it goes, absolutely correct, and is a truly marvellous
example of the direction which modern science is
taking in the person of one of its highest representatives.
It would almost seem as if the chasm between the
"superstitions of the past" and "exact" science is
about to be bridged over.

In a lecture given a year later at the Royal
Institution, he pictures

"the action of two forces on the original protyle,
the one being time, accompanied by a lowering
of temperature, the other swinging to and fro like
a mighty pendulum, having periodic cycles of ebb
and swell, rest and activity, (but) it is evident a
third factor must be taken into account.   Nature
does not act on a flat plane ; she requires space
for her cosmogenic operations, and if we introduce
space as the third factor, all appears clear . . . .
Let us suppose the zigzag diagram (Professor
Emerson Reynolds') not drawn upon a plane
but projected in a space of three dimensions,
what figure can we best select to meet all the
conditions involved . . . . , inasmuch as the
curve has to pass through a point neutral as to
electricity and chemical energy twice in each
cycle ? . . . . A figure of eight (8), or lemniscate . . . . fulfils every condition of the
problem.   If we project this figure in space, we
find, on examination, that the points of the curves

where chlorine, bromine, and iodine are formed
come close under each other ; so also will sulphur,
selenium, and tellurium ;   again, phosphorus,
arsenic and antimony, and, in like manner, other
series of analogous bodies. It may be asked whether
this scheme explains how and why the elements
appear in this order ?   Let us imagine a cyclical
translation in space, each evolution witnessing the
genesis of the group of elements which I previously
represented as produced during one complete
vibration of the pendulum.   Let us suppose the
one cycle has been thus completed ; the centre of
the unknown creative force, in its mighty journey
through space, having scattered along its track
its primitive atoms—the *seeds*, if I may use the
expression, which are presently to coalesce and
develope into the groupings now known as
lithium, beryllium, boron, carbon, nitrogen,
oxygen, fluorine, sodium, magnesium, aluminium,
silicon, phosphorus, sulphur and chlorine.   What
is most probably the form of track now pursued ?
Were it strictly confined to the same plane of
temperature and time, the next elementary
groupings to appear would again have been those
of lithium, and the original cycle would have been
eternally repeated, producing, again and again,
the same fourteen elements.   The conditions,
however, are not quite the same.   Space and

E

electricity* are as at first, but temperature has altered, and thus, instead of the atoms of lithium being supplemented with atoms in all respects analogous with themselves, the atomic groupings, which come into being when the second cycle commences, form, not lithium, but its lineal descendant potassium. . . . Each coil of the lemniscate track crosses the same vertical line at lower and lower points . . . . Dominant atomicities are governed by the distance (backwards and forwards) from the neutral centre line, monatomic elements being one remove from it, diatomic, two removes, and so on. In every successive coil the same law holds good."

Is this a new discovery, or was it ever known before? One of the "superstitions of the past" was a belief in the magic virtues of the Caduceus. The form was modified by the Greeks, but the original Caduceus of Hermes (the Egyptian Thoth, the Hebrew Enoch, the greatest of the Hindu Seven "Pitris" or enlighteners) was a rod entwined by two serpents.

---

* If we might, with all due respect to the learned Professor, suggest a correction, we would substitute the term "polarity" for "electricity." The successive spirals, represented by the lemniscatory series, are known to mediaeval occultists as the "Seven Fires," of which electricity is one. Polarity, however, is a constant factor in the whole series. This accounts for the number fourteen in the elementary groups. It is very remarkable how the septenary doctrine is forcing the hand of modern science.

Everyone knows the form of the Caduceus, and what is it but a lemniscatory series? It was the symbol of Magic (or wisdom), because magic is that art by which man, recognising the essential identity of his own spiritual nature with the forces that lie behind the phenomenal universe, becomes able to produce similar phenomena on a small scale. " No one," says Madame Blavatsky, "will deny that the human being is possessed of various forces ; magnetic, sympathetic, antipathetic, nervous, dynamic and mental, and that they are all biological in their essence ; the physical intermingling with, and often merging into, those forces which we call intellectual and moral ; the first being the vehicles, as it were, of the second. Their presence and co-mingling are of the very essence of our being ; they are not suppositions and abstractions, but realities, and the only active realities whose attributes can be determined by direct observation."* In spite of all atomo-mechanical theories by which scientific material- ists hope to avoid the plain issue of the divisibility or indivisibility of the atom, the fact remains that the whole science of Occultism is built on the doctrine of the illusory nature of matter.

I have now dealt as briefly as possible with the three Axioms, not, of course, with the idea of *proving* them, but for the purpose of shewing that they possess

---

* " Secret Doctrine."

no inherent improbability, inasmuch as they are supported by a large mass of evidence, and witnessed to by a large number of persons who would indignantly repudiate any attempt to impose dogmatic utterances, in the shape of axioms, as a basis for scientific investigation.

LECTURE III.

꒐T is related in the Talmud that Rabbi Eliezer-ben-Orcanaz having replied unsatisfactorily to certain questions propounded to him concerning his teachings, the doctors present refused to admit his conclusions. Thereupon Rabbi Eliezer endeavoured to convince them of the truth of his doctrines by causing a karob tree to rise from the ground and transplant itself a hundred cubits away; a rivulet to flow backwards; and, finally, the Great Bath-Kol, or voice from Heaven, to say, "What are the opinions of all the Rabbis compared with the opinion of Rabbi Eliezer?" Then arose Rabbi Joshua, and said, "It is written 'the law is not in Heaven, it is in your mouth and in your heart.' When, therefore, Rabbi Eliezer has proved to us that karob trees, rivulets and unknown voices afford us reasonings equal in value and weight to that reason which God has placed within us to guide our judgment, then we will admit their testimony and estimate them as Rabbi Eliezer requires."

If this wise advice had been followed by Christians, much time and energy would have been diverted into more useful channels than profitless attempts to prove that the Christian revelation must be true because our Lord and His Apostles worked what are called "miracles."

These "evidences" of Christianity, as they are called, are not only useless, but sometimes even mischievous, as, for example, the arguments from "design," etc., to prove the existence of God. Their very plausibility was a real danger until the scientific doctrine of evolution revealed their superficial nature. Of course, God does not *ex*ist, He *sub*sists; otherwise He would not be God.

This, it may be said, is Pantheism, but Pantheism, like all other false, or rather, defective systems, is right in what it asserts, and only wrong in what it denies—viz., personality which Pantheists (who, like the man in the German proverb, are unable to see the forest for the trees*) hold to be excluded by the doctrine of immanence.

The doctrine of God's immanence in the cosmos is, however, essential to Christian monotheism, and has the authority of S. Paul himself, who made effective use of it in combating the agnosticism of the Athenian philosophers which, like modern materialism, was based on atomo-mechanical conceptions, or rather misconceptions, of the universe. The great error of Pantheism is that it takes the reflexion of God in Nature for Himself, and thus lays itself open to the charge of atheism. Evolution, which is progress from imperfection to perfection, cannot be predicated of

---

* Er sieht den Wald für Baumen nicht.

the Divine Being, Who can never be otherwise than perfect. Of God, in His essence and absolute Perfection, we can, and do, know nothing, but only His reflexion in time, which is the medium of illusion. There can be no evolution of God Himself, but our human conceptions of Him the Cause are, in themselves, of the nature of effects, and the *effect* is the unfoldment of the *cause* in time. But we may speak of the evolution of the God-*Idea*, or man's conception of Him, which proceeds apace with man's own intellectual and spiritual evolution. Now, the God-Idea, like all other phenomena, is the result of vortical action, for the same law prevails in the intellectual and spiritual as in the physical world. This, however, requires explanation. "How," it may be said, "can ideas and spiritual concepts be spoken of in terms of motion?" In this way : our conceptions of force on the physical plane arise from motion, and motion is that which increases or diminishes the distance between one object and another. Now as distance is a term which can be predicated of abstract ideas—the distance between love and hate for example,—we may speak of that which increases or diminishes the distance between separate ideas as motion on the intellectual plane. Accordingly, if motion in the physical world implies physical force, we may use the term intellectual force to denote that which causes motion in the world of ideas. Again, motion implies direction, which involves the idea of space, and time is, of course, an element in every conception. Given then time, space and force on the mental plane, and vortical, or any other kind of motion, may be predicated of mental concepts. If, therefore, it be a universal truth that all phenomena are the result of vortical action, what may we expect to find when we endeavour to trace the course of the evolution of the God-Idea ?

And here it is necessary to call attention to one or two facts. I have said that the evolution of the God-Idea proceeds apace with man's own intellectual and spiritual development. God is that which we shall be eternally in process of knowing, and at every fresh stage, former ideals of the Supreme Being appear grotesque, and we wonder how they can ever have been entertained by intelligent men. It is only necessary to refer to the horrible figment of Calvin, and the " Three Lord Shaftesburys in one Lord Shaftesbury " of the last generation, as examples of that fatal religious empiricism whose inevitable tendency is the establishment of a rival devil successfully disputing the Divine Supremacy. In considering, therefore, the evolution of the God-Idea, we must bear in mind that the thinking nations of the world belong to the Aryan, or fifth, period of this planet, corresponding to the period of maturity in the individual man or the microcosm ; and we may expect to find, therefore, that so far as God can be apprehended by the intellect, or fifth principle, man will attain to that apprehension before its close. The fuller *spiritual* apprehension of God requires faculties which are yet in embryo, and is reserved for future stages of man's evolution, when he will enter on the period of his decline of earth-life, and preparation for a higher consciousness.

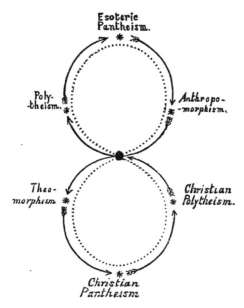

Let us see, then, whether the law of the double vortex, or lemniscate, holds good on the intellectual, as well as on the physical plane. The above diagram will illustrate my meaning. Round the dotted figure of 8, which stands for the evolution of the God-Idea in the Fifth Root Race, are seven arrows, numbered 1, 2, 3, etc., representing the seven stages of progression, and corresponding roughly to the sub-races. I say roughly because, for our present purpose, it is necessary to indicate these stages definitely, and it would land us in inextricable confusion if we endeavoured to trace the evolution of the God-Idea in any given sub-race without taking into account all the various and complex forces which go to form the intellectual life of the tribes and nations of which it is composed. But, roughly, we may say the seven stages in the Root Race correspond to the intellectual growth of the seven sub-races in their order. The black disc in the middle of the figure represents the neutral centre of ignorance, corresponding, in Mr. Crookes' scheme, to the " point neutral as to electricity and chemical energy." The evolution of the God-Idea starts from this neutral centre, arrives at the same point half-way in its evolutionary course ; and touches it again at its finish. But ignorance is of two kinds, the ignorance of hope and of apathy ; and it is the latter which characterises the ignorance of the materialistic or fourth period. Intellectual materialism seeks to dignify it by calling it " agnosticism," and even " scientific agnosticism," which, if it mean anything, means that ignorance of God is the beginning of wisdom. We shall, however, deal with this phase of evolution in its place. The arrows, representing the seven stages of progress, point in their order to six asterisks which indicate the prevailing religious tendencies of the respective periods. It must not, however, be assumed that the advance proceeds with unimpeded regularity. It resembles the ebb and flow of the tides of the sea, rather than the steady progress of a river—hence the difficulty of assigning to any given sub-race a particular form of religion. A sub-race is composed of many nations whose intellectual life is dependent on so many and various accidents, such as geographical position, physical type and development, etc., as to preclude the attempt to label it with any approach to accuracy. Besides, the element of degeneration has to be taken into account. Degeneration is now a recognised fact in science, and, as a writer in "Lux Mundi" has well observed, it "acts more powerfully in religion than in any other region. Religion never rises above its last reformer until a new one appears.

Take, for example, the period represented by arrow 4. It may be said to begin with the return of the Jews from Captivity, and to be drawing towards its close at the present time. Before the Captivity, nothing is more noticeable in the history of the chosen people than their strong tendency to Polytheism. The reason is that they

were surrounded by degenerate offshoots of the
nations who had survived the periodical cataclysm
which paved the way for the evolution of the Fifth
root race.   In spite of the restrictions imposed
on them by the Mosaic Law, marriages were, from
time to time, contracted with the surrounding
heathen, and this hybrid element in the nation
contributed powerfully to its degeneration, and the
people, on whose life the fate of the whole race
depended, was dying fast.   The Captivity was their
salvation.   For a time they ceased apparently to
exist, but during that time a wonderful change was
wrought.   They came into contact with a still
vigorous branch of the Fourth root race, over whose
intellectual life a wave of Aryan influence had
flowed. It was about that period that the followers
of Sakya Muni experienced a fierce persecution
from the adherents of the unreformed Brahminism,
which terminated in their expulsion from peninsular
India.   The votaries of Buddha fled eastward and
northward, planting in some of the Hindu-Chinese
nations their religion under Brahminical forms, and
in others, engrafting their contemplative Theism on
the prevalent idolatries; for, in Buddhism, there
has always been an esoteric and an exoteric doctrine, the former of which is capable of adaptation
to any existing religious system.   There can be
little doubt they also fled westward to Babylon,

for we recognise them in the " Brachmani," of whom frequent mention is made both in the later philosophical and the ecclesiastical writings. S. Clement of Alexandria mentions Buddha by name as "honoured by the Brachmani as a God, on account of his virtue."* Had they been adherents of the *old* Brahminism, they would certainly have reported nothing good of Buddha.

The captivity must have cut the Jews to the heart. As they "sat by the waters of Babylon and wept when they remembered Zion," their case seemed hopeless. But a remnant of the nation survived the fiery ordeal, and when, at the end of 70 years, they returned to the land of their fathers, every vestige of their old tendency to idolatry had been obliterated. Formerly they gravitated towards polytheism. Now their monotheism was ineffaceable. But, as I shall endeavour to show later, a distinct advance had been made during that period in the evolution of the God-Idea. The crude anthropomorphism of the pre-captivity era was modified by a Pantheistic element of Aryan origin, which was subsequently engrafted on the old stock and bore fruit in the Kabbalah and Alexandrian mysticism.

Let it be understood then, that though the God-Idea evolves through seven forms in the Fifth Root Race,

---

* Strom. i, sec. 15.

and that they correspond roughly, in their order, to the evolution of the seven sub-races, the former is an intellectual, and the latter a physical evolution. The septenary law prevails on both planes, but it cannot be expected that *all* the laws which govern the intellectual region should co-relate *accurately* with those by which purely physical phenomena are regulated. We shall endeavour, therefore, to trace the evolution of the God-Idea with only occasional reference to the correspondence of its stages with the seven sub-races.

A glance at the diagram will reveal a rather curious fact, viz., that while arrows 1 and 2 mark a steady advance in the intellectual apprehension of God, arrow 3 seems to indicate. a retrograde motion, for no one will deny that anthropomorphism is *intellectually* a distinctly lower conception of God than Pantheism. The close of the second stage marks the period of the highest civilization in India some thousands of years before the Christian era, and I have given it the name of " Esoteric Pantheism," because, while Brahminism is a polytheistic religion for the multitude, it is founded on a philosophical system which is essentially Pantheistic. Hitherto the evolution of the God-Idea had been a purely intellectual one. It was, so to speak, the discovery of God in His aspect of Unconditioned Cause. But the personal, and with it, the moral element was lacking and in order that the evolutionary track should not return into itself, an impetus in a fresh direction was necessary. It will be remembered that, in Mr. Crookes' scheme, the lemniscate is projected in a space of three dimensions, the planes of the two curves not coinciding. To produce this figure it is necessary to postulate three forces : the centripetal and centrifugal for the curves, and a lateral force for their angular incidence. In the physical evolution of the elements, this third factor is represented by a *lowering of temperature.* Can we find anything corresponding to this in the evolution of the God-Idea ? If the term "intellectual temperature" be admissible, does history point to any event which would seem to indicate such a condition at any given period ? Now, whatever may be said in favour of the policy of isolation which was the key-note of the Mosaic legislative system, it was certainly not calculated to promote intellectual growth in the people who submitted to it. Material prosperity was the reward of obedience, and the punishment of disobedience was disease, or destruction at the hands of their enemies. Of a future state, or life beyond the grave, they do not seem to have formed any idea in the pre-Captivity era ; and, in later times, the sect of the Sadducees appealed triumphantly to the Law and the earlier Prophets as affording no authority for the belief of the Pharisees in a spiritual world and spiritual beings.* It seems, at first sight, curious that the people, on whom depended the intellectual and moral future of the whole race, should develope a civilization so grossly material. They carried neither science nor art one step forward. The second commandment froze up art, and all scientific inquiry was checked by the answer, " things are thus and not so, because Jehovah wills it." As to the wisdom of Solomon and the magnificence of the first Temple, there can be little doubt that both have been grossly exaggerated. Otherwise, it is a most extraordinary fact that the Jewish nation over whom, but a few hundred years before, the mighty Solomon had reigned in all his glory with a magnificence scarcely equalled by the greatest monarchs, spending millions of money on a temple, was overlooked by the historian Herodotus, writing of Egypt on one side and of Babylon on the other, visiting both places, and of course, almost necessarily passing within a few miles of the splendid capital, which, like the Phœnix, had risen from its ashes. And if Solomon was remarkable for his wisdom, it must be remembered that, in his old age, he went after other gods, and was probably initiated into their mysteries.

How, then, was Jewish anthropomorphism an advance on Hindu Pantheism? It was not an intellectual

---

* Josephus says that the Sadducees rejected all the books of the Old Testament except the Pentateuch, but there would seem to be some doubt about this.

advance at all, but a moral one. For the first time in the history of the Fifth Root Race, the idea of God was inseparably connected with the idea of righteousness, and the intellectual evolution received a temporary check from the lateral force of a spiritual revelation, the effect of which was to alter the angular incidence of the lower evolutionary curve. It was the revelation of the Divine Personality in its aspect of Unity, and a preparation for the fuller revelation of the WORD MADE FLESH and the Christian doctrine of the Trinity in Unity, which alone is capable of reconciling the seeming contradiction between immanence and personality.   Thus the apparently retrograde movement was, in reality, a step forward ; for while monotheism, in its lowest form of anthropomorphism, is scientifically grotesque ; in its highest it has this advantage over pantheism, viz., that it is incapable of being "defecated to a pure transparency." Monotheism, in fact, is a spiritual revelation.   It is quite a mistake to suppose with most theologians, that "primitive man" worshipped one God.   Primitive (material*) man worshipped the ghosts of his ancestors, and polytheism as Mr. Herbert Spencer shews, was the next development.   Abraham was the first monotheist, for the pre-

---

* Man did not become material until the third Root Race. The fall (or descent into matter) marked the beginning of his intellectual evolution on this plane of consciousness. This will be explained later.

F

Abrahamic period of Jewish history must be relegated
to the region of symbol and myth ; and to him, as
the father of the chosen people, was imparted the
revelation that there is one Supreme God. But the
revelation of His Name was reserved for a later
period, and was vouchsafed to a man better fitted
by education to receive it than the half-civilized nomad
chief. It was to Moses, " learned in all the learning
of the Egyptians," that God revealed His name of
Yah-veh (or Jehovah), which corresponds to the Hindu
" Manu-Svayhambuva " or self-existent, with this difference, that *Yah-veh* involves the idea of personality.
We learn from Exodus v. iii. that by this name He
was not known to Abraham, Isaac and Jacob. The
name, it is true, frequently occurs in the book of
Genesis, but it is the opinion of Calmet and most
other commentators, that it is used there by anticipa-
tion. Now this marks a very important step in the
evolution of the God-Idea. The name given to God
by a nation implies the character of its own moral
development, but this Name being given to the Jews
as a revelation involves, of course, elements of thought
beyond what they had attained to. This name dis-
tinguishes the true God from all false ones. It is well
said by Dr. Kay (" Crisis Hupfeldiana," p. 9), that " in
that oft recurring phrase ' Yah-veh your Elohim ' it is
clear that we could no more transpose the words than
in the expression " I am Joseph your brother " . . .

*Yah-veh,*though etymologically signifying self-existent, yet, as being the *personal* name, gathered up into association with itself whatever attributes were manifested in God's condescending intercourse with man, especially therefore His righteousness, faithfulness and mercy."

But, as the intellectual evolution from ancestor worship to Pantheism was a gradual process, so also was the evolution of the idea of God's Personality. Anthropomorphism was naturally the first step, and communication was always through the "angel of Jehovah," of whom we shall treat further when we come to speak of the celestial hierarchy. The anthropomorphic element is, indeed, inseparable from the idea of personality, and its evolutionary culmination in the "Word made Flesh" is a witness to its necessity as a means whereby man may be brought into his true relations with God. To this next development I have given the name "Theomorphism," which marks the close of the fourth period, and this, as I have said, brings us to quite modern times. Theomorphism is the worship of the Divine Man; and here we find ourselves face to face with the difficulty before mentioned. It is almost impossible to correlate this period at all accurately with the history of the fourth and fifth sub-races. In what are sometimes called the "ages of faith," when the fourth sub-race, or the

Latin nations of Europe, were the leaders of religious thought, Christ was undoubtedly worshipped as God. But the doctrine of the Holy Trinity, apart from which Theomorphism would have no *raison d'être*, was a dogma of the schools ; and, throughout the middle ages, it manifested a constant tendency to degenerate into Tritheism, which is a step backwards in the direction of anthropomorphism. This tendency shewed itself in the art of the period in which God the Father is frequently represented as an old man with a flowing white beard, seated on a throne, and holding before Him the crucified Redeemer, while a white dove, symbolical of the Holy Spirit, hovers above. Degeneration reached a further stage in the spurious Trinity of the Father, Mother and Son, of which mediæval art furnishes several examples. On the other hand, modern Theomorphism inclines to the opposite extreme of a shadowy Pantheism, and for this reason I have placed it midway between the fourth and fifth period. The fifth sub-race may be described roughly as the English-speaking people. Of course it contains fourth, and even third, sub-race elements, but few will deny that religious thought has shifted its centre of gravity in modern times, and that it is to English, rather than Latin Christianity, that we must look for further development of the God idea. The evolutionary tide wave has receded from the fourth sub-race, and the

Latin nations of modern Europe exhibit a strong tendency towards scientific materialism, against which the Church, deprived of her former power and influence, can only feebly protest. But in England materialism has spent its force. The tide is advancing, and has already checked the flow of the backward current. The tendency towards materialism which, ten or fifteen years ago, characterised English science in the person of its highest representatives is now a thing of the past. "Huxley" and "Tyndall" are no longer names to conjure with, and, indeed, aggressive scientific materialism may be said to have died with Professor W. K. Clifford. It must, however, be admitted that much of the current agnostic speculation on the existence of a "First Cause" is still tainted with materialism. When Mr. Herbert Spencer, e.g., defines the "Unknowable" as a "power manifesting through phenomena" and "an infinite eternal energy," it looks as if he were only able to grasp the physical aspect of being, or the energy of cosmic substance. That cosmic energy may have for its cause cosmic *ideation* does not seem to have occurred to him, and there can be little doubt that this one-sided mode of dealing with the problem is largely due to the pernicious practice of subordinating consciousness to the things of which consciousness takes account, and regarding it as a bye-product of molecular action.* Be that as it may, it is beginning

---

* "The Secret Doctrine," vol. 1, p. 327.

to be pretty well recognised, in England and America, that materialism has said its last word, and that if we wish for a satisfactory explanation of the Universe, science must look in another direction. With the decay of materialism has disappeared much of that hostility to religion which, until quite recently, characterised the attitude of the leaders of scientific thought. On the other hand, the leaders of religious thought—in the Church of England at any rate—so far from regarding scientific discovery in the light of an enemy, are willing, and even anxious, to claim it as a friend and ally.* With Christianity, on its moral side, science has no quarrel, but as sacramentalism—or the recognition of the principle that the *noumenon* is the reality and the *phenomenon* the illusion—does not yet commend itself to the scientific mind as a working theory of the Universe, which, like evolution, may be a basis for a new departure in its methods of investigation, the claims of Christ to Divinity are disregarded.

Accordingly, we find that while the religion of the

---

* In a magazine called the "Agnostic Annual" (Stewart & Co., 41, Farringdon Street, E.C.) a Mr. B. Russel, presumably an agnostic, writing on "The New Anglicanism," refers to "Lux Mundi" in the following terms :—"It is a confession of faith from the younger and rising leaders of the High Church party (who are) the salt of the Church. Whatever of enthusiasm, whatever of sainthood, whatever of self-sacrifice, whatever of scholarship, whatever of poetic feeling the Church of England possesses, finds its best expression in the High Church party. The Anglo-Catholic revival has done everything for the Church. And the

fifth sub-race is distinctly Theomorphic, its science exhibits a strong tendency in the direction of Pantheism. But the religious and intellectual evolution of the sub-race are both converging to the point of sacramentalism, and when that point is reached, and the pioneer of scientific sacramentalism appears, the fifth period of the evolution of the God Idea will draw towards its close, and Christian Pantheism will put an end to the conflict between science and religion which has lasted so many centuries.

Of the next development, or "Christian Polytheism," I propose to treat in the following lecture, which will deal with the Celestial hierarchy.

---

book ' Lux Mundi' is the intellectual offspring of the men *who will presently be the sole leaders of this party.* . . . For here, from the stronghold of dogma, without the abatement of one iota of the claims of sacredotalism and sacramentarianism, are suddenly held forth concessions of the highest importance to the spirit of reason, theological liberalism, and nonconformity. The book is . . . less an unwilling concession wrung out by the inexorable logic of facts than an enthusiastic statement of the new doctrines, and a triumphant avowal of their assimilability by orthodox theology.'' ("Agnostic Annual," 1891.)

LECTURE IV.

3N the preceding lecture I endeavoured to show how the revelation of the Divine Unity acted as a lateral force on the cyclic evolution of the God idea, projecting it in a fresh direction and round another centre. It started as a purely intellectual process, and the first coil of the lemniscate had for its centre the human reason. But "the world by wisdom knew not God," and if further progress was to be made a new centre was necessary. In the fulness of time the Divine Man appeared. The God idea had evolved through the successive stages of Polytheism, Pantheism and Anthropomorphism, and had arrived once more at the neutral centre of ignorance.

Now whatever opinions may be held in regard to the Person of Christ—whether He was Divine, or human, or semi-human, or præter-human, or, as the Catholic Church has always maintained, God and Man, "yet not two but one Christ"—it will not be denied that His appearance in the world marked the close of one intellectual epoch and the beginning o another. Pre-Christian speculation about God wa essentially teleologic. It was an endeavour to accoun for the existence of man and the phenomenal Universe and it reached its highest intellectual point in Hind

Pantheism. But the moral element which, in modern times, is recognized as essential to the conception of God, was conspicuous by its absence, and it was not until that period was drawing towards its close that we recognize in the writings of Plato the first shadowy indications of the necessity of a moral centre for any further development of the God-Idea, and of the existence of such a centre nature afforded no proofs. The neutral point of ignorance was again reached and man was without God or hope in the world when suddenly a great sign appeared. A Man was born in an obscure province of the Roman Empire who claimed to be Himself that centre. We are not concerned at present with the defence of this claim, but merely point out that it has been found impossible to ignore it. The most "liberal" of modern thinkers shrink from charging with audacious imposture the founder of an ethical system which compels their admiration, and Whose life was the highest recorded manifestation of the Religious Ideal. Accordingly the ingenuity of those who are unable to accept His claims to Divinity, has been taxed to the utmost in the endeavour to explain them away. That He was a great moral teacher no one denies, but that His Person has "a metaphysical and *cosmical* significance"* is an idea repugnant to an age so impatient of the supernatural as our own. But

---

* Martensen Christl. Dogm. sec. 128.

it has to be taken into account, and accordingly, the interest of modern physical enquiries into the laws of the cosmos or the origin of Man is immediately heightened when these enquiries are suspected to have a bearing, however indirect, upon Christ's Sacred Person. The evolution of the God-Idea in the pre-Christian era, consistently with its teleologic character, had for its centre the human reason. But this is now felt to be inadequate to meet the altered conditions of the problem. So long as the evolutionary track was confined to the intellectual plane, the centripetal force of reason maintained the necessary equilibrium. But the lateral spiritual impetus introduced a new element, that of righteousness, as essential to the conception of God, and the centrifugal force of scientific enquiry, which would otherwise expend itself in a tangential direction in its endeavour to compass the Infinite, is held in equilibrium by the Personality of Christ. A personal centre has this great advantage ; that its sphere of attraction is not limited to the intellectual plane, but is able to control the centrifugal force of speculation about God whether it take a physical, intellectual, or moral form. Accordingly, under the Christian dispensation, belief in God may take any form that is not inconsistent with believing "*rightly* the Incarnation of our Lord Jesus Christ," and this constitutes the claim of the Christian religion to Catholicity. Belief in God can only take three forms, polytheism, pantheism, or anthropomorphism, and the doctrine of the Holy Trinity is alone capable of blending into a synthetic unity these apparently irreconcilable ideas. The worship of the Man-God satisfies the anthropomorphic instinct which differentiates religion from philosophy. The sacramental idea, which is involved in the doctrine of the " Word made Flesh," is essentially pantheistic; while polytheism, or the recognition of diversity in Unity in teleologic research is redeemed from the charge of idolatry when the principle laid down by S. Paul (I Cor., ch. viii.) is admitted, that though "there be gods many and lords many," yet (for us), there is but "one God and one Lord ;"—that is, all secondary causes have their origin in the one great Cause to Whom alone supreme worship is due.*

It is with this polytheistic element in Christianity that we have now to deal, and it may be as well here to anticipate two objections that may be raised against the existence of any such element. The first is a religious objection, viz., that polytheism, or

---

* This interpretation may be objected to on the ground that in verse 4, S. Paul says, "we know that an idol is nothing," but it is evident he means nothing to Christians, for in chapter x., v. 20, he says that the Gentile sacrifices are offered to " devils " and warns his converts against partaking of such food *knowingly*. S. Chrysostom, commenting on I Cor., viii., 5, says, " for it seems that there are *really* several gods " (see De Mirville " Des Esprits," vol. II., p. 322).

the recognition of inferior deities, even if such exist, is contrary to the spirit of Christianity, and is distinctly forbidden in Holy Scripture, inasmuch as it tends to obscure our relations to the Supreme Deity. There is much force in this objection. The danger was formerly very great and has not yet wholly ceased. Communion with higher intelligences *may* lead to the sin of idolatry unless certain conditions are observed. As I am not writing for initiates but for ordinary Christians, I may as well say at once that they should never be approached except through the Sacrament of Holy Communion; or in terms officially authorised by the Church in the case of Roman Catholics. On the other hand, I may be allowed to point out that the question of a polytheistic element in Christianity is, at present, of scientific interest only. We have not yet arrived at that stage of the evolution of the God-Idea in which it will have a religious significance.

The second objection is that the existence of inferior deities is a purely gratuitous assumption. "Granted," it may be said, "that the physical universe has its origin in that which is not physical, why should we seek to differentiate the Unknown Cause?" The answer is, because the logical sequence of analogies in the evolution of beings demands it. We are obliged to conceive of the Supreme God, on the one hand, as a purely spiritual essence, exalted above all that is finite; and on the other, as having a definite relation to the created universe. Now creation involves intention, desire, thought, work ; and these are properties that imply limit and therefore belong to a finite being. And, moreover, the imperfect and circumscribed nature of this creation precludes the idea of its being the direct work of the Infinite and Perfect. The solution of the problem lies in the Christian revelation of the Word made Flesh. A revelation, as I have said, is the unveiling of a hidden truth, and that this is a truth is proved by the fact that on no other intelligible hypothesis can the existence of the Universe be accounted for. Let us examine it.

Of God's nature in Itself we can and do know one thing only,—that it is transcendent Love. Now love is the manifestation of self to that which is not-self. How then is the love of the Father revealed ? In and through the Son who, by manifesting in time, returns the love of the Father by revealing it, for otherwise the Love of God would be manifest only to Himself. The Son is therefore the Cause of the universe, or, as S. John puts it, "All things were made by Him and in Him was life," for " the effect is the unfoldment of the Cause *in time*."* We may regard the Universe, then, as a theophany, or the externalization of the Divine Love.

The question then arises, " by what process does

---

* Vide infra.

the love of the Eternal manifest in time ? "   " The *life*
of the Word," says S. John, " is the *light* of men." The
Son, therefore, by limitation becomes the Divine Reason, or the connecting link between the relative and
the absolute.   In the Kabbalistic " Book of Zohar "
the principle is thus formulated, "All that is has its
origin in the Ain Soph " (or Divine Wisdom).   " But
the idea is at first undeveloped; it lies enfolded within
itself.   When the idea begins to expand, it arrives at
the degree of *spirit,* then it takes the name of *intelli-*
gence (or the reason of the creature), and is no more, as
before, hidden, the idea has externalized itself."   Accordingly it is through the " Sephiroth," or intelligences, that the "Ain Soph " issues ultimately in the
plastic principle of the material Universe.   It is here
that the polytheistic element in Christianity comes in,
for the idea which is popularly held of creation as the
making of something out of nothing is absurd, and irreconcilable with the omnipresence of God.   Matter is a
mode of force, force is a mode of will, and will is a
mode of intelligence.

 The Sephirothal series of the Kabbalah, however,
is open to one grave objection.   It takes no account
of the element of illusion which is necessarily implied
in the theophanic doctrine ; for the Universe is not
real because it is not *eternal.*   God is the only Reality,
and the Kosmos is a reflection of Him, as it were, in a
mirror.   Pantheism takes the reflexion for the reality,

and thus lays itself open to the charge of atheism. In dealing, therefore, with the process by which the Eternal manifests in time, I prefer to adopt the Dionysian series, which not only has the advantage of being in accordance with Christian tradition, as probably derived from S. Paul himself, but meets all the conditions required. Dionysius the Areopagite, said to have been consecrated by S. Paul bishop of Athens, has always been regarded in the Christian Church as the great authority on the celestial hierarchy, and is referred to by Dante in his vision of Paradise as

> " . . . . quel cero
> Che, giuso in carne, più addentro vide
> L'Angelica natura e'l ministero."*

It is true that modern criticism assigns a later date to the writings which, at one time, were directly attributed to him, but this is of little consequence. Pseudepigraphy was formerly a very common method of embodying tradition, and there is no reason to doubt that the unknown compiler has fairly dealt with the materials of which he was in possession.

In these writings we have, collected and focussed, all extant traditions in regard to the celestial hierarchy, and the system thus elaborated is not only in harmony with modern thought, but does not run counter either to Holy Scripture or to the Christian view of the re-

---

* Il Paradiso, Canto x., v. 115.

lations between God and man. According to the Dionysian scheme, there are nine orders of celestial beings, and grouped in triads, they correspond to the Brahminical "Trimurti" or Elements in the developing process by which the material universe was evolved out of pure spirit.

1st Triad.	2nd Triad.
SERAPHIM (Σεραφιμ)	DOMINIONS (Κυριοτητες)
CHERUBIM (Χερυβιμ)	MIGHTS (Δυναμεις)
THRONES (Θρωνοι)	POWERS ('Εξουσιαι)

3rd Triad.

PRINCIPALITIES (Αρχαι)

ARCHANGELS (Αρχαγγελοι)

ANGELS (Αγγελοι)

The first triad cannot properly be termed separate beings, but rather Divine faculties or emanations. They correspond to the "Adi Buddha" of the Indian mystics, and represent the sum total of all the spiritual energy and wisdom in the Universe. Just as the brain is the centre from which radiate numberless faculties—physical, intellectual, and æsthetic,—so the Seraphim and Cherubim and, in a less degree, Thrones must be regarded as the primal outward manifestations of the Deity. They belong to the region of absolute con-sciousness, or *duration* as distinguished from *time*, for time is that which produces illusion. What we call the

present is only a mathematical line dividing that part
of duration which we call the future, from that other
part which we call the past. The real person or thing
is for us composed of the sum of all its various and
changing conditions *as it passes through our plane of
consciousness.* "No one could say that a bar of iron
dropped into the sea, came into existence as it left
the air and ceased to exist as it entered the water,
and that the bar itself consisted only of that cross
section thereof, which at any given moment coincided
with the mathematical plane which separates, and at
the same time joins, the atmosphere and the ocean."*
Even so, the sense of actuality which we derive from
this succession of momentary glimpses of any person
or thing is an illusion, for it is only, as it were, a cross
section of the reality. The Seraphim, then, represent
the Divine Love in its absolute consciousness, the
Cherubim, absolute Divine Wisdom, and Thrones, the
absolute Divine Sovereignity.† The last in the series
"Thrones," connect the first with the second triad.
It must be borne in mind that we are here dealing
with modes of existence that are utterly transcendental, and accordingly, when we say that "Domi-
nions" are the first *objective* manifestation of the *sub-*

---

* The Secret Doctrine, vol. I., p. 37.

† We must be careful not to confound the Dionysian Seraphim
and Cherubim with the theophanic "Angels of Presence," which,
in Hebrew literature, these names are sometimes used to denote.

G

jective Divine Sovereignty and collectively the male principle of the cosmos, we must not be understood to mean more than they belong to the region of relativity, that is, they are *existences* on the highest plane of consciousness or pure spirit. "Mights" (Δυναμεις) correspond to the Indian "Mula Prakriti" which is primordial substance, or pure force on the plane of spirit. It is the noumenon of all phenomena on every plane of relative consciousness, and is, so to speak, the matrix, or female principle, of the Universe, which is the fruit of the mystic union between Prakriti and *Purusha*, or pure undifferentiated spirit, The last order in the second triad are "Powers." This, however, is a very inadequate rendering of the word Ἐξουσιαι which denotes objectivity. They are the only ones, in this group who, in any human sense, can be said to exist objectively ; and are of two kinds, the Powers of Light, and the Powers of Darkness. Of the latter I propose to treat in a succeeding lecture in connexion with the origin of evil and the mystery of the Eighth Sphere. The Powers of Light are the "Elohim" (gods) of the first chapter of Genesis, who speak in the first person plural (Let *us* make man in our own image),* and the seven spirits (or breaths)

* It is quite a mistake to suppose that the plural form has any reference to the Holy Trinity. One of the unhappy results of the admission of the "Filioque" clause into the Nicene Creed without œcumenical authority, has been the tendency, in western theology,

of God mentioned in the Apocalypse. They are, in a certain sense, the creators of the world ; that is to say the world proceeded from them, for, as we have seen, the idea which is popularly held of creation as the making of something out of nothing is absurd, if for no other reason than that it is inconsistent with the doctrine of the omnipresence of God. Each of the seven breaths is correlated to the seven-fold occult forces of nature operating on different planes of consciousness, and these occult forces are correlated, in their turn, to potentialities inherent in every human being, but of the nature of which the large majority of men are totally ignorant. I am precluded, however, for obvious reasons, from enlarging on this head. The creator of the material world was Jahve (or Jehovah) the Lord of form. And here it is necessary to correct an error so widely prevalent that the very notion of its being an error will fill many people with astonishment. It has somehow come to be taken for granted that Jehovah is the First Person in the Holy Trinity, and yet there is not the faintest shadow of

---

to "divide the substance" of the Holy Trinity. The use of the terms Creator, Redeemer, Sanctifier, to signify respectively the Father, the Son and the Holy Ghost is most misleading. If by the Son, all things were made, why should the Father be considered as the Creator? and, if, on the other hand, the Holy Ghost be the Lord and Giver of Life, the life which is *in* the Son (S. John, I. 4) is derived from the Holy Spirit, eternally proceeding from the Father to Whom the term Fount of Deity rather than Creator may be more properly applied.

authority for such a statement from beginning to end
of Holy Scripture. S. John expressly states that by
the WORD all things were made. Our Lord said to
the Jews "Your father Abraham rejoiced to see *my*
day and was glad (S. John, VIII., 56). Everything
points to the fact that God always reveals Himself,
whether as Creator, Redeemer, or Sanctifier, in, by
and through, the WORD, nor is it possible to conceive
of any other way in which the Eternal could manifest
in time. The manifested Logos is called by the
Hindus " Iswara " (the Lord), or the highest consciousness in nature, and is a compound unity of
manifested living spirits, plus their divine *reflexions*
on the plane of illusion.

Thus it is that the Powers of Light (Maha Buddhi),
though one in their essence, as the manifested Logos,
are reflected in *time* as seven, which emanate from, and
return into, the Logos, each in the culmination of its
time. Of these seven, Jahve is the lord of form. The
other six preside over the evolution of beings who
exist in what is called the region of " Arupa loka " or
the formless. No further information on this head can
be given, as such knowledge pertains to the higher
mysteries, and can only be conveyed in words which,
as S. Paul says (speaking as an initiate), " it is not lawful to utter."

As God by the Word created all things, so the
Word, by Jahve, created the *universe of form*, and

revealed Himself as Man to man. In the book of
Genesis, a clear distinction is made between the work
of Jahve and the work of the collective Elohim. And
both are distinguished from El-Yon, the Supreme, or
Most High. We read (Deut. xxxii.) that when the
Most High separated the children of men the LORD
(Jahve) *took for his portion* Israel, Jacob being the *lot*
of his inheritance. The theophanic angel of the Lord
was Michael whose name signifies "like unto God,"
and he was the Jewish national deity, or *Prince* of
Israel. And here we touch the fringes of a great
mystery. Though our Lord Jesus Christ took not on
Him the nature of angels, yet "in Him dwells all the
fulness of the Godhead." Though "raised far above
Principalities and Powers," He manifests through
them in virtue of that fulness. We may, therefore,
regard Him as displaying, under the Jewish dispensation, the activities which are represented by these
celestial orders. S. Paul teaches clearly (Gal. iii. 19)
that the Law was of angelic origin, and Clement of
Alexandria says, "Formerly the Word was an angel,
but, . . . the Word has *appeared* and that mystic
angel is *born*,"—or has taken on Him the *nature of man*.*
Of course, by the term "angel," he means the theophanic reflection, and this brings us to the third group,
—Principalities, Archangels and Angels. Though the

---

* Paed. Book I. ch. 7. See also Justin Martyr, Apol. 6 and 63,
and Tryph. Dial. 34, 56, 60 and 93.

term "angel" more properly belongs to the lowest order of the celestial hierarchy, the ministering spirits and guardians of individuals, it may be, and in point of fact is, taken to signify all the spiritual beings of the third triad, for they are actual *existences* with intelligence and free will. They are neither pure undifferentiated spirit, nor, exalted though it be, is their consciousness absolute, or unconditioned by time. The Principalities, though collectively omniscient, are not omnipotent. Their will power is irresistible, but, as we shall see when we come to treat of the Principalities of Darkness, irresistible will, plus omniscience, is not the same thing as omnipotence. The Archangels are not omniscient, though their knowledge transcends all human conception, and by their wisdom the nations of the world are guided, each in its appointed order fulfilling its part in the evolution, physical, intellectual and spiritual, of the human race. But they have never fathomed the lengths and depths and heights of the manifestation of the Divine Love, and before the mystery of the Incarnation they veil their faces and cry " Holy, Holy, Holy." The Angels are not omnipresent, for though they are not subject to the limiting conditions of space,* their sphere of action is this world : and their office is the ministry to individual man of the Divine Love which embraces all creation.

---

* Hence their symbolic wings.

It will be observed that the functions of the third triad are inverse in the order of dignity when compared with the first. The highest Divine faculty, Love, is represented by the highest order Seraphim ; Cherubim, or Divine Wisdom, come next, and Thrones, or Sovereignty, last ; whereas, in the third triad, the Angels "or ministers of Love" are the lowest, the ministers of Wisdom are higher, and the ministers of Will, higher still. The reason of this is because they are *existent* beings.

God, as we have said, is the One Reality, and the Kosmos is His reflection. Let me not be misunderstood, however. Reality is that which Is. But the human criterion of reality is objectivity, and things are subjective or objective according to our states of consciousness. The highest truths have, for those who can realize them, an objective existence ; the grossest material forms have no existence for him who cannot perceive them. For us, the real is that which we can *realize*, or objective existence, and accordingly, the third triad is real in the sense of being objectively existent, and only unreal in the sense which it shares with all creation of being, not God, but His reflection in *Maya* or the medium of illusion.

I will now deal as briefly as possible with the functions of the third triad. Principalities may be described as the angels of periods. It is very difficult to convey a clear idea of the nature of their activities,

but the task must be attempted. Every age has, so to
speak, its own idea or *Zeit Geist*. Now it is a common-
place that ideas rule the world. But it is not generally
known that they derive their potency from the spiritual
force which lies behind them, and prepares the world
for their reception. Was Luther the cause of the
Reformation? In a sense, undoubtedly he was. But
if Luther had been born in the tenth century, he would
have lived and died an obscure monk. On the other
hand, the sixteenth century could not have passed
without some great religious convulsion. Men do not
cause the *Zeit Geist*, they co-operate with it. All
great movements in the external world are the results
of battles, fought and won, in the spiritual region. A
conflict, in which innumerable hosts have been en-
gaged, finds its ultimate expression in half-a-dozen
human organisms who, over-shadowed by the victors,
become the leaders of a new movement. Of this, however, I shall treat presently in connexion with the
Archangels. To the order of Principalities belongs
the mysterious being called Satan, whom it is a mistake to confound with the Devil. To this confusion
may be traced the controversy as to whether the Devil
is or is not a person. Strictly speaking, the Devil has
no existence in the sense that cold has no existence.
It is the absence of heat. But to refuse to take account
of the Devil in theology is as unreasonable as to refuse
to light fires in the winter because science teaches that

there is no such thing as cold.   Satan, however, or the *manifestation* of the Devil, is a personality and the usurping king of this planet.   But he is not, as Milton taught, and it is generally supposed, a fallen archangel, like Beelzebub, Mammon, etc.   We are expressly told by S. Jude that the Archangel Michael recognized his superior dignity, in that he durst not bring against him a railing accusation.

Archangels are generally described as "angels of races." But this gives us only a very imperfect idea of the functions assigned to this celestial order which are not always subject to ethnic limitations.   In what are called the "Canonical Scriptures" only two are mentioned by name,—Michael and Gabriel (the latter belongs to the theophanic class), but in the book of Enoch, which is accepted as canonical in the Abyssinian Church, we find the names of several others, such as Phanuel, Surakiel, and Raguel, and these are not angels of races, but of departments of human activity in all races.   Thus, Phanuel presides over repentance, and the hope of those who will inherit Eternal life, and Surakiel, over those who transgress the moral law. This is very curious and suggestive of the way in which God "orders the unruly wills and affections of sinful men," by the establishment of a spiritual hierarchy with due relations of control and subordination whose office it is to resolve into harmony the discords of the world and, in its entirety, constituting what is called

Divine Providence.* Archangels are the Dhyan Cho-hans of the Oriental religious systems, and are of two kinds, the ascending and descending. The former are the advanced entities of previous great cycles, who, having perfected themselves beyond the highest limit consistent with any given condition of planetary life,—our own for instance,—pass on to the Dhyan-Chohanic condition. Others there are who, evolved out of the infinite womb of Prakriti, or the Mother principle of Nature, are coursing towards the outermost limits of existence. With this distinction, however, we are not now concerned, but with another ; their division into good and evil angels, between whom there rages an in-cessant conflict. I have said that all great movements in the external world have their origin in the spiritual world, and that the conflict of ideas which marks the transition period between one historical epoch and another is, as it were, a copy of a battle already fought and won in the spiritual region. On such a transition period we have just entered. The reader may take the following facts for what he thinks they are worth.

---

* It is to be hoped that the Church of England will, at some future time, see her way to re-admitting into her Canon of Scripture the long lost and lately discovered Book of Enoch. It is most valu-able as supplying materials for a theory of the universe which will harmonise with modern thought. The fact that it was not written by the patriarch Enoch, as was generally supposed until the time of Origen, is no reason why it should be excluded, any more than the Epistle to the Hebrews, or the Book of Daniel, on the grounds of doubtful authenticity.

The year 1879 marked the close of an epoch in the intellectual life of Europe and America. In that year, the hosts of light, under S. Michael the Archangel, obtained a decisive victory over the hosts of darkness, led by Beelzebub and Mammon,* in a series of battles extending over a period of thirty or forty years. About the middle of this century, the Fifth Root Race touched the point known to occultists as the point of physical intellectuality, or the lowest in its evolutionary cycle. Its upward progress, if it is to preserve its cyclic path, must be in the direction of *spiritual* intellectuality. It is very difficult to convey to the ordinary reader the meaning of these terms which, it must be confessed, are rather clumsy. Physical intellectuality, however, may be described as the tendency to regard as unreal all that is incapable of definition and measurement by human standards. It is a period of limits and boundaries, of mechanical authority in religion, of

---

* Beelzebub has been called the "God of flies." Disease germs would be more correct. The life of these microscopic creatures which are the cause of zymotic disease, and indeed, all forms of parasitic life, vegetable as well as animal, are determined by lunar influences and are consequently under the control of the Lord of the Eighth Sphere. This is well known to those who practice in the higher kinds of evil magic or sorcery. Mammon (whose name is derived from the Syriac word for riches) is one of the "rulers of the darkness of this world" (Eph. vi. 12). He is the god of "barriers," and presides over all those evil influences which are begotten of ignorance, prejudice and fear. It is for this reason that he is supposed to be specially connected with material wealth, as constituting a false standard of worth and dignity.

atomism in science, and of individulism in politics.
Spiritual intellectuality is all that physical is not ;—
freedom of thought in religion ; pneumatism (if I may
coin a word) in science, and socialism in politics.

On this period we have, as I have said, only just
entered.   In the spiritual region the battle has been
fought and won, but some years must elapse before its
effects begin to shew themselves plainly in the world.
Two men, however, have been born out of due time,
and a third will shortly appear.   John Worrell Keely
in America, and Tolstoi in Russia are pioneers of the
dawning era ; and both will share the fate of men born
a century too soon, viz., obloquy, persecution and
failure.   But "he that hath ears to hear, let him hear"
the trumpets of the Archangels announcing their
glorious victory over the Prince of this world whose
second judgment (or crisis) has come.   Yet a third, and
he will be overthrown and bound 'for a thousand ages.

We now come to those beings properly termed
angels, or ministering spirits.   This word "ministering" has giving rise to some confusion of thought.
An idea prevails that the angels are all *our* ministers
or servants, but this is a mistake.   Even the appointed
guardians of individuals minister *to* God *for* us.   They
are called in the original "λειτουργικα πνευματα" and
the adjective implies Divine Service.*   Our authorised

* One word "liturgy," or the service of the Altar, is derived
from the same source.   In Greek, λειτουργειν is to say Mass.

version is also responsible for another error, viz., that the angels are pure spirit, and also of a fiery nature. Angels are not pure spirit, they are spirit plus soul, and only one class can be properly called fiery. It all arises from a mistranslation of Psalm civ. 4. The proper rendering is " Who maketh the winds his messengers and flames of fire his servants." The author of the Epistle to the Hebrews has taken a clever advantage of the LXX. version to press this text into his service. He cannot be accused of dishonesty as the word πνευμα signifies equally wind or spirit and αγγελος is the same as messenger.

The angels, then, are dual in their nature, as are all created beings except man, being spirit and soul. All creatures below man, whether animals on the material plane, or those beings which we call immaterial because the matter of which their bodies are composed is imperceptible to our senses on account of its tenuity, (and which are known as " Elementals ") are soul and body.* Man alone is a trinity, or the image of God. It has sometimes been alleged as a reproach against the unfallen angels that they are will-less, but this is not strictly correct. It must be remembered that, as repre-

---

* The Elementals are sometimes called " Nature Spirits ;" the term "spirit" being often used loosely to designate immaterial intelligences. Strictly speaking they are not *spirits* at all, for they have no moral responsibility, but only will and a very automatic kind of intelligence. The Angels are the true Nature Spirits.

sentatives to the individual of the Divine Love which embraces all creation, they are spiritually automatic, and cannot be otherwise without losing their purity. To this danger, however, they are in reality liable at a certain stage in their evolution, and when that moment arrives, their latent will-power will assert itself in a direction which cannot be named, as knowledge of this kind belongs to the higher mysteries.

We have now to consider how far communion with the angelic host, or CHRISTIAN POLYTHEISM, is lawful ;—in other words may we pray to them without falling into the sin of idolatry ?

We may regard prayer as a form of spiritual energy, having an intellectual value, and capable of being expressed in terms of will, as will-power is a form of vital energy, possessing a mechanical value, and capable of being expressed in terms of motion. Now the difference in the effects produced by a given quantity of energy on the physical and intellectual planes is apparent if we compare the value of a day's work by a bricklayer's labourer, and a man of science. In the same way, those who are acquainted with the laws of psychical dynamics, know that the work produced by a fixed amount of energy on the intellectual plane is, in turn, enormously inferior to that produced on the plane of spirit. The words "*laborare est orare*" contain a profound truth. If then, to pray is to labour on the spiritual plane, who can tell what results may not

follow from communion with those unseen intelligences who, in the order of God's Providence, stand
in direct relation to the hidden forces of nature, and
wield the powers intrusted to them in conformity with
the Divine Will ? If it be true that innumerable
multitudes of angelic beings fulfil the commands of
the Almighty, as responsible agents, in administering
the affairs of this and other worlds, the great difficulty
of reconciling prayer with the reign of law disappears.
For, on the theory of the Universe which we have
been considering, law is not the result of blind inexorable force, but of *cosmic ideation.* Prayer may be
regarded, therefore, as the translation into will power
of spiritual energy, and is part of the machinery, so to
speak, by which the universe is governed.

Perhaps no kind of prayer has been the subject of
more ridicule than prayers for rain or fair weather.
But whom is it intended to crush—children who pray
that it may not rain on a holiday ? " No ! " thunder
our scientific meteorologists, " but the clergy of the
Church of England, with the Archbishop of Canter-
bury at their head, who know, or ought to know, that
the state of the atmosphere is regulated by laws which
have no possible connexion with the desires of any
individual or set of individuals." But is this really so ?
We know very little of the laws which regulate atmos-
pheric conditions beyond the fact that dryness and
humidity in the air are caused by variations in local

temperature which, in turn, depend largely on terrestial magnetism. But what is magnetism ? A mode of energy. But will-power is also a mode of energy. Are our scientific men prepared to assert definitely the absence of any common value between the two, such as is admitted to exist between magnetism and other forms of energy,—heat, electricity, etc. ? Is it so very unscientific to believe that the desire of a whole community, concentrated on this particular object, may possibly liberate forces which may not be without influences on terrestial magnetism ?—let us say by vibratory coincidence.* Of course, in our present state of knowledge, or rather ignorance, of the laws of nature, they are not justified in assuming more than the bare possibility that such may be the case, but in the absence of any proof to the contrary, the charge of superstition cannot be maintained.

Prayer, then, being the liberation of spiritual energy, it is a question, not only of theological, but of scientfic interest, to whom should it be addressed. Let it be remembered, in the first place that Christian Polytheism, or the recognition of and communion with those "gods many and lords many" who, like ourselves, live, move and have their being in the Great Unconditioned Cause, is *not* idolatry, so long as we maintain

---

* If Keely's "Motor" should ever become an accomplished fact, who can tell what marvellous results in the future may not follow from the application of the law of vibratory coincidence ?

a firm grasp on the truths enshrined in the Creeds. On the contrary, paradoxical as it may sound, it is really a safeguard against that sin. For what is idolatry but the rendering to another of that supreme worship which is due only to the HOLY and UNDIVIDED TRINITY. It has even been ruled irregular by several councils of the Church to address our prayers *to* Christ, instead of *to* the Father, *by* the Holy Ghost, *through* Christ. This seems very strange to modern Christians who are accustomed, for the most part, in proportion to their devoutness, to concentrate the whole of their devotion on the Person our Blessed Lord. Indignantly as they would repudiate Sabellianism in words, it cannot be denied that many good people, in their anxiety to avoid the Arian Scylla, manifest a tendency in the direction of the Sabellian Charybdis.* Be that as it may, angel worship is the traditionary antidote against anthropomorphism, which is not only a grotesque and degrading conception of the Supreme Being, but utterly incompatible with a right belief in the Holy Trinity. For the very highest conception that we are able to form in our *minds* of a Great First Cause falls immeasurably short of the real dignity of even an Archangel, and to render Divine homage to such a

---

* In the Roman communion this tendency is very marked. Devotions are encouraged, such as the Cultus of the "Sacred Heart" which an orthodox Christian of the third century would have regarded with considerable suspicion.

H

being is to rob God of His due.   Are we then denied
access to God the Father because our mental faculties
cannot rise to the conception of Him?   A thousand
times No! Through Christ Who is the express Image
of the Father, we have this access in the Sacrament of
His Body and Blood. The more perfectly our human
life is assimilated to the Divine Life the more clearly
will the Father be revealed not *to* us but *in* us. It is
not intellect but love which reveals the Father, and in
the filial love and obedience of the Perfect Son the
revelation is full and complete. The ministry of His
Law is committed to the Angels, the ministry of His
Love, which is Himself, to His Blessed Son. But if
the Angels are ministers of the Divine Law, we are
surely justified in rendering to them that inferior
homage which has always been claimed for them by
the Catholic Church upon principles plainly elementary to the relations of one being to another. And if, as
we have seen, prayer is the liberation of spiritual energy,
communion with the angelic host, whatever form it
takes, must resolve itself ultimately into the orthodox
"*Ora pro nobis.*"   For as the operations of spiritual
beings who are influenced by prayer are also on the
spiritual plane, they will fall under the same category.
Of course there are dangers to be avoided.   The pursuit of truth is ever attended with danger.   But with
our feet firmly planted on the rock of the Creed, there
is no real ground for apprehension lest the contempla-

tion of the celestial glories, which are revealed in the ministry of the angelic host, should so dazzle our spiritual vision as to make us forget that their exalted activities have their source in the Lord and Giver of Life, to Whom with the Father,—the Fount of Deity, and the Son,—His express Image,—the ONE HOLY and UNDIVIDED TRINITY, is alone due the supreme worship of every creature.

LECTURE V.

M Y task this evening is a difficult one. The truths which I shall endeavour to convey are fragments of knowledge pertaining to some of the very highest mysteries, the full comprehension of which requires the development of faculties wholly latent in the majority of human beings, and but very feebly developed in the West, even among initiates. It will be my duty to explain, to the best of my ability, certain facts in connexion with a mystery known as the Mystery of the Eighth Sphere, which is a key to the problem of evil in the Universe. It is sevenfold, and each of its minor mysteries is correlated to the sevenfold mystery of Life on their seven planes of consciousness Now I am well aware that there are many occultists who say the subject ought not to be brought before the public at all, and object to the very name being mentioned, and some of them have been endeavouring to alarm my good friend Mr. ——, who has cautioned me to be careful whom I admit to these lectures. In reply to such persons, it is due to myself to say I am breaking no oath, and violating no confidence. These lectures were advertised in the public journals, and all who choose to attend them are welcome. I regret to be obliged to differ from many persons, whom I hold in the highest respect, as to whether or not the times are ripe for mentioning these subjects. They have been mentioned,—prudently, or imprudently,—and are familiar to all who have taken an interest in the Theosophical movement. What is more, they are being thought about, and I am convinced, in my own mind that, under the circumstances, the continuation of the policy of total silence, hitherto observed, is *less* prudent than guarded speech. When we consider that an immense mass of knowledge has already been made public which, though to all appearance, frozen at its source, must inevitably thaw in the coming century, I humbly submit that it is wiser to dig trenches than to risk a devastating flood. The first person, however, to profane the mysteries (albeit unconsciously) was Mr. Sinnett, the author of "Esoteric Buddhism," a book which made considerable sensation when it came out, but which contains nothing new that is true, and nothing true that is new. As he was the first to make public the information that there is an "Eighth Sphere" and a mystery connected with it of which he is ignorant, it may be as well to say that both these statements are true. But when he proceeds to say that the Eighth Sphere is the moon, he gives utterance to one of those half-truths that are more misleading than falsehoods. As well give, as a definition of man, the aggregate of the chemical constituents of a decomposing body.

The mystery is indeed the mystery of Death ; it

is sevenfold,* and each of the seven mysteries is correlated to the sevenfold Mystery of Life on the seven
planes of consciousness.

Readers of " Esoteric Buddhism " will remember
that man is said therein to evolve on seven planets;
three of which (including the Earth) are visible, and
the other four composed of matter too attenuated to
be visible.   Also that there is an eighth planet,—the
moon, in which matter "asserts itself" yet more
strongly than on the earth.   Anything more utterly
misleading it is impossible to conceive.   Madame
Blavatsky, who knew very well that this kind of thing
was sure to be exposed sooner or later, has, in her
" Secret Doctrine," corrected some of the errors, but as
she has not chosen to elucidate any portions of the
Mystery except such as suit her purpose, and as she
is destitute, moreover, of the literary gifts of her dis-
ciple, her teaching in respect to the Seven Planets and
the Eighth Sphere will be "*caviare* to the general,"
who will continue to regard Mr. Sinnett's explanation
as the genuine " Esoteric Buddhism."   If my audience
will kindly bear in mind that the esoteric doctrine is
no more the peculiar property of Buddhists (Thibetan

* In connexion with one of these, from the point of view of
occult chemistry, if I may use the term, the Moon might, perhaps,
be called the eighth sphere. Of course no occultist recognizes such
a science, though the lowest kind of witchcraft is, in a certain
sense, an occult chemical operation.

or European) than the moon itself, I will endeavour to throw what light I can on the subject.

In the first place, the only visible planet on which man evolves is this earth. He never inhabited Mars, or Mercury, or any of the visible planets, or was connected with any except the Moon before it became a satellite. Every other planet in the Solar System is ruled by its own " angel of periods," and the evolution of the lower kingdoms of nature (animals excepted) is proceeding on them (or in connexion with them) at different rates, in accordance with a law known as the law of acceleration and retardation. The fact of a planet being visible only shews that the fourth, or Mineral kingdom, is at its fourth stage of evolution at such or such distance from the Sun. But, though man has nothing to do with Mars or Mercury in this sense, he has been connected in the past with three other worlds and will in the future inhabit three more which, with the earth, will make seven. It is also true that an evolution of the lower kingdoms of nature is proceeding at different rates on the earth and what may be called its " companion " globes, to distinguish them from the planets proper. These companion globes are of course invisible, for they are all either above or below the material plane.*

---

* The words "globe" or "sphere" are very clumsy, for it is only in a metaphorical sense that they can be used to denote the centres of attraction in the highest and lowest stages of man's evolution. (See next lecture).

The next thing to be remembered is that everything exists in two alternating states, which may be described as manifesting, or *active*, and unmanifesting, or *potential.* The Sanscrit words "*manvantara*" and "*pralaya*" are as good as any to denote these states, so we may as well use them. It should be borne in mind, however, that they are relative to the planes on which they occur. For example, when a human being is born into the world, he enters on his "manvantara" of earthly consciousness, and on his "pralaya" as regards his former state. Similarly, when he dies, he is in "pralaya" to the earth and in "manvantara" to the world of super-physical concepts which, by the way, is not "Devachan."*

Now in order to understand the nature of man's evolution on earth and its companion spheres, we must first ascertain his relation to other forms of life. Every planet, as I have said, is ruled by its own angel of periods, and every period is a concrete manifestation of cosmic energy which represents the evolution of a kingdom of nature at a certain rate which we may call x. Man—the highest kingdom—is the highest manifestation of cosmic energy in nature (for the angelic

---

* "Devachan" is the only Thibetan word used by "Esoteric Buddhists" but they have utterly perverted its meaning. It is regarded in Thibet as a kind of ante-chamber to Nirvana. The Buddhists of Peninsular India do not recognise this state, and the Thibetans hold that from Devachan returns to the earth are impossible (Schlagintweit Buddhism in Thibet, p. 102). Evidently the "Mahatmas" are heretics.

hierarchy are *super*-natural, and belong to the realm of cosmic ideation). But every kingdom of nature contains within itself a certain proportion of all the others, potentially or actively, which are taken up in turn at each round on every successive globe of the chain, commencing with the second. For example, man is now evolving on the fourth globe of his planetary chain, on which he has arrived for the fourth time. On the three preceding rounds he was amorphous, for he only contained *potentially* the forces which have enabled him, at his present state of evolution, to subject to the law of his own being the law of chemical affinity, which is a law of the fourth, or mineral, kingdom. The human body is an impossible chemical compound, for no sooner has the man cast it off than decomposition sets in. During his physical life, the law of chemical affinity is controlled by the higher biological law of selection and assimilation ; and here, having cleared the ground of a multitude of misconceptions, I will endeavour to explain what the Eighth Sphere really is. To do so we must go very far back in the history of the cosmcs. Otherwise we shall be met by the objection that the existence of an Eighth Sphere is contrary to Axiom I.

I said in the last lecture that the second triad in the celestial hierarchy (or trinity of generation)*

---

* The three triads are (1) the triad of the Absolute, called in Sanscrit "*Sat*" which can only be translated by the clumsy word "Be-ness,"—(2) the triad of Generation, corresponding to the Kabbalistic "Macroposopus," and—(3) the triad of *Maya* or illusion, viz., that which is conditioned by time.

is composed of the male principle (Maha-puruṣha or pre-cosmic ideation), the female principle (Mula-prakriti or pre-cosmic substance) and their offspring the Elohim, or Creators ; the highest beings, as we have seen, who can be spoken of as *existing* or capable of being differentiated from Absolute Being. Now the very essence of *existence*, or manifestation, is duality, hence, they are .divided into two classes, the Powers of Light, and the Powers of Darkness.

And here we find ourselves face to face with the great problem of the Origin of Evil, and how to reconcile its existence with the goodness of God. To the question "Why does God permit Evil ?" the theologian, strong in faith, but weak in knowledge, returns the correct but irritating reply " For His own glory." What is required, however, is a solution of the problem, and not an answer delivered *ex-Cathedrâ*. Unfortunately, the theologian, directly he begins to attempt a solution, falls into a pit at the very first step, the pit of "dualism," which has been the curse of theology from the age of Augustine up to the present time. From this catastrophe a little knowledge would save him. Two is not, nor can it be, a symbol of perfection, for it implies difference or contrariety. Monotheism and Polytheism are both tenable systems teleologically, but Di-theism is utterly absurd and unworkable. On the other hand, two is the symbol of manifestation, or subjectivity and objectivity, and it is in the recognition of this fact that the solution of the problem of the origin of evil is to be found. Absolute Good cannot, in the nature of things, be manifest except to Itself. To all finite conceptions relativity is necessary. We can only know light by comparing it with shade, and good by comparing it with evil. There can be·no such thing as absolute evil, for it would be the negation of absolute good, which is God. All evil is therefore relative, or conditioned by time, which is the medium of illusion, and is the negation of *relative* goodness. But relative goodness is imperfection, and the negation of imperfection is perfection. Therefore evil is perfection, or God, which is absurd. But God is the All in one, therefore if evil be not God, it is nothing. Q.E.D. "Why callest thou me good?" said the Master, "there is none good but One, that is God." "Be ye perfect as your Father in heaven is perfect." Let theologians who wish to understand the mystery of evil ponder these two sayings, for in the reconciliation of them the solution lies. "Free-will" is an *ignis fatuus*, a deceptive light, and those who follow it will, sooner or later, find themselves in the *cul-de-sac* of fatalism or the pit of dualism.

It is not, however, with the metaphysical, so much as the historical aspect of the problem that we have now to deal. The cosmos is temporal, as I have said, in its aspect of manifestation to finite intelligences ;— that is, it had a beginning, or an evolutionary stage be-

hind which we cannot go ; the former stages being unthinkable, though not on that account less *real*. The
present cosmic manvantara is the manifestation of the
Divine Love. It was preceded by the cosmos of
Divine Wisdom which lived, moved and had its being
on a supernatural plane of consciousness, and culminated in a race of exalted beings who manifest collectively in the new era as the Elohim or Powers of
Light. But, as we have seen, manifested light implies
darkness. What then are the Powers of Darkness?
If evil be imperfection, they are imperfect manifestations of the Divine Wisdom. If you will bear in mind
the Oriental division of the Dhyanis, or celestial beings,
into two classes, the ascending and descending, you
will recognize the Powers of Darkness as entities on the
ascending arc of this cycle of Divine Wisdom which they
had not completed before its period of pralaya had set in.
But as they had progressed too far to be thrown back
into the vortex of a new primordial evolution, they
return, during the cosmic pralaya, to their static condition and remain as a latent force until the next
cosmic manvantara, when, at a certain stage of its development, they mingle with the progressed entities of
the new period and complete their evolution vicariously.

It is here that a certain law called the law of acceleration and retardation produces equilibrium in a way
that I will presently explain. The law of a and r
may be thus stated. All evolution proceeds in cycles.

During the first half of each cycle, its rate is subject to a gradual diminution which, if the initial velocity be represented by x, culminates in $\frac{x}{7}$. It then increases in the same proportion that it diminished, its final corresponding with its initial velocity ; the whole series being expressed in multiples of seven. Let us remember that the Dhyanis of the former period were on the *ascending* arc of their cycle, and complete their evolution in *this* in an ever-increasing ratio of acceleration, whereas the Dhyanis who had already completed their cycle, and manifest in the new period as the "Elohim" or "Powers of Light," were subject to the law of retardation, being on the *descending* arc of the new cycle.

Now the forces on different planes of consciousness which go to make up man ultimately resolve themselves into two vortices which represent his higher and his lower nature, and if we take the lemniscate for his symbol, in pursuance of our method, his relation to cosmos, in accordance with Axiom II. will be represented by the following figure,

the larger curve symbolizing the macrocosm, and the
smaller, the microcosm. How is this figure produced?
It is the result of three forces.* Each coil is composed
of a series of spirals representing, in their turn, the
elements in the developing process whereby the
noumenal becomes the phenomenal. But the point
of intersection is a dead centre, and a third factor is
required by the conditions of the problem. For the
point of intersection corresponds to the will, or the
middle principle between the higher and the lower
nature, and in order that the point may become a
circle (or manifest) it requires to be crossed by the
axis of a fresh vortex at another angular incidence.
Now this circle is in reality a *sphere*—the Eighth
Sphere ; but it cannot be expressed in other than two
dimensional terms consistently with the illustration
which is necessarily imperfect. The lemniscate is
projected in three dimensional or phenomenal space,
whereas the cosmogenical operations of nature are not
thus restricted, but extend into what is known as
the "region of permeability." For this reason the
"Mystery of the Eighth Sphere" must always remain

---

* The occult formula of Being (*sub*sistence and *ex*istence) is "The
one becomes two,—the two, three,—and the three, seven." One is
the symbol of the Divine Essence which is Unity, and two is the
symbol of manifestation. $1+2=3$, or God in manifestation—the
Holy Trinity. Two multiplied by itself is 4, the symbol of generation or the cosmos. $4+3=7$, which is the perfect number—the
All, or God and the Universe.

a mystery to the uninitiated, and even to the initiated below a certain grade, as its comprehension requires the development of perceptive faculties latent in the majority of men.

In Mr. Crookes' scheme of physico-genesis, the difficulty is surmounted by the introduction of the element of temperature, a lowering of which produces contraction. But temperature is itself an effect of motion in the region of permeability, so that even the physical genesis requires that the "third factor—space" be "accompanied by (a fourth) a lowering of temperature." Still, however imperfect the illustration may be for our present purpose, and only shadowing forth, as it were on a screen, the outline of the reality, it may assist us to apprehend somewhat of the Mystery of the Eighth Sphere, so far as its operations come within the range of intellectual process.

Let us first consider what is called the "torsion of impact," or the effect produced when two vortices meet whose axes impinge at an angle. If the medium of the two be of equal density, and their velocity be also equal, they coalesce and form a parabolic figure, but if their velocity be not equal, they form two conical spheroids revolving in opposite directions, corresponding to the figure of 8 which we have selected as the symbol of man's evolution. This, it will be seen, meets the conditions involved, for it will be remembered that the ascending Dhyanis of the former period complete their evolution, in this cosmic manvantara, under the law of acceleration, whereas the Dhyanis who manifest as the Powers of Light are on the *descending* arc of their cycle, and are subject to the law of retardation. Accordingly, the vortices which respectively répresent their activities, are of unequal velocity.

We have now arrived at that portion of the Mystery which relates to the moon. It is expressed technically thus—" When the macrocosm and the microcosm meet for the fourth time at the point of intersection, four (the cosmos or generation) is wedded to five (the evil number),* or, as Madame Blavatsky would say, when man has completed the third round of his planetary chain and begun his fourth, the centrifugal force of the new vortex, acting in the mineral, or fourth kingdom of nature, projects into space a portion of globe *d* (or the fourth in the chain) which revolves round it as its satellite. Madame Blavatsky in her " *Secret Doctrine* " makes a great point of the fact that the moon is older than the earth, and that Jehovah is a lunar deity. It is difficult for any one who knows the truth, to read this part of her work, without admiring the extraordinary ability, but at the same time noting the extraor-

---

* The pentacle reversed is a favourite figure with black magicians who use it to concentrate their will currents and project them with fatal effect against those whom they wish to injure. It is intimately connected with lunar influences and is the symbol of parasitical life.

dinary unscrupulousness with which she contrives to
insinuate that Jehovah is the god of impurity and
grossness, and his adversary the true benefactor of
mankind.   It may be admitted that Jehovah-Michael
was the god of human generation, and that his number
is 4 (the tetragrammaton), and that his adversary was
Lucifer the light-bearer and lord of human wisdom.
But is generation an evil thing?   It is blasphemy to
assert it, a "doctrine of demons" as S. Paul says.
For generation is the last expression of Love on the
material plane.   Whatever of impurity or grossness
attaches itself to the idea is mind-born.   Shakespeare
uttered a profound truth in the person of Hamlet when
he made him say " There's nothing good or bad but
thinking makes it so."   Adultery and fornication are
bad because they are disorderly.   *Corruptio optimi
pessima.*   All disorder in the external world springs
from cyclical aberration on the plane of spirit, and the
author of cyclical aberration is the light-bearer in his
character of Sathanos the adversary—the usurping
prince of this world.   For it must be remembered that
Lucifer Sathanos belongs to the order of Principalities,
and his period is the evolution of human reason.   It
may be asked why the Powers of Darkness manifest in
the person of the light-bearer?   The answer is because
they manifest on the plane of illusion.   The light over
which they preside is human reason, and it is deceptive
because all reasoning is conditioned by time, or the

I

medium of illusion.   It is, however, only a question of degree.   As all evil is imperfection, and absolute evil the negation of God, or nothing *(asat)*, so absolute darkness is not, and cannot be, except during a cosmic pralâya.

This is apparent from the allegory of Genesis. When the Elohim said " Let there be light " it was necessary in order that the light should be manifest to divide it from the darkness.   Accordingly, they made (manifested as) two great lights, the Sun to govern the day, and the Moon to govern the night.   Now this must not be taken to mean the material sun and moon, for it has reference to a period ages and ages before the Universe existed in a material form. The Sun stands for the collective Elohim and the moon for Jahve-Elohim reflecting in the person of the "Angel of the Lord" the divine Light of the Sun of righteousness until the period of His manifestation. And now we see why Jehovah was a lunar Deity. Emanating from the Logos, or Being on the highest plane of consciousness, he manifests in the person of his angel, until the culmination of his period, which is the period of darkness or illusion.   S. Paul, as an initiate, well understood this, but he was precluded from stating it otherwise than indirectly.   Hence his laboured attempt, in the epistle to the Romans, to demonstrate that we are not under the law by which sin came, working "all manner of concupiscence.

"For I know" he says (Rom. vii. 18) "that in me, that
is in my flesh, dwelleth no good thing." His fellow
apostle might well say " our beloved brother Paul hath
written many things hard to be understood, which the
unlearned . . . wrest to their own destruction,"* for
in the seventh chapter of his epistle to the Romans he
seems to contradict himself over and over again. What
his argument really comes to is this. Man has a higher
and a lower nature ; and in the lower nature there is a
law of " concupiscence " (kama-rupa) warring against
the higher,—the " inward man " or true self. But God
is the author of the lower, as well as of the higher,
self. Did God then create sin ? No, he says, for
"without the law sin was *dead*" (v. 8) but "when the
commandment came, sin revived and I died " (v. 9).
God, then, is not the author of sin, but of the law,
which was " ordained " he says elsewhere (Gal. iii. 19)
" by angels in the hand of a mediator." But why was
it ordained if, though in itself "holy, just and good,"
the consequence was evil ? In order, he replies, that
sin " might *appear* sin," or become manifest. In other
words, the point of intersection in our symbolical
lemniscate, which represents the will, or middle principle between man's higher and lower nature, ex-
panded into manifestation under the centrifugal impetus caused by the impact of the fresh and more rapid

* 2nd Peter iii. 16.

vortex which was set up by the ascending Dhyanis of the former period hastening, under the law of acceleration, to complete their evolution vicariously in the new cosmos. This was the first fall, or descent into matter, of the angels who mingled their essence with the most progressed of the material forms into whom Jahve had "breathed the breath of life" (Gen. II., 7). The will of man became manifest, therefore, by the evolution of his reason, and the immediate effect was the knowledge of good and evil. "Behold," said Jehovah, "the man has become as one of us" (the Elohim). "Now, lest he take of the tree of life and live for ever," *i.e.*, lest he evolve into spirituality under the law of acceleration, "therefore Jehovah sent him forth from the garden of Eden to till the *ground* from whence he was taken." From which it is evident that the garden of Eden was not on earth at all. The Mahometans have a tradition which is singularly near the truth; namely, that the garden of Eden was in the middle region between the earth and the moon, The facts are these. Differentiation on the plane of spirit precedes differentiation on the physical plane, and is from the lowest to the highest kingdom of nature. At the time of the "Fall," Man had assimilated to the laws of his own being the three (elemental) kingdoms of nature which precede the mineral kingdom. He was a descending Dhyani at the fourth stage of his evolution, or, as Madame Blavatsky would say, had

evolved for the fourth time on the three first globes
a, *b* and *c*, of his chain, and had commenced his
evolution on *d*, the fourth,—our earth. Now every
kingdom of nature corresponds to a "principle" in
man, and every principle, as I have said before,
is correlated to a principle in the cosmos. The
fourth principle in the cosmos is the Divine Will,
and by it man evolved his fourth principle (*kama rupa*,
·or "body of desire") on the three planes of consciousness below the physical plane. Now in accordance
with Axiom II., the first three stages of his evolution
on the physical plane were a reproduction, microcosmic in point of time, of his evolution on the three
preceding planes, just as the individual human fœtus
during the few months that elapse between conception
and parturition, runs the whole gamut of evolutionary
progress from mineral to human being. Accordingly,
when man first appeared on this earth, he was *materi-
ally* undifferentiated—the Adam Kadmon of the Kabbalah. He had not descended into matter, and it was
at this time that the vortices manifested in· macrocosm
in the mineral kingdom, causing a projection into
space of a portion of globe *d*, which then became
the vehicle of his body of desire. Let us be very careful to remember that this is a projection in *space*, and
in no way affects the shape of the symbolical lemniscate, for it takes place at the *point* of intersection.
The centrifugal and centripetal forces which give birth

to the spirals of which the figure is composed are not on the physical plane, and only touch it at that point. The spirals which represent his lower principles converge towards, and those which represent his higher diverge from, this point, and are respectively above and below the physical plane, for as above stated, the conical spheroids, resulting from the impact of two vortices of unequal velocity, revolve in opposite directions. The point, then, towards which man tends in the first half of his evolution, and from which he rises in the second, is *maya* or illusion. His "body of desire," therefore, or the faculty by which he comes into relation with the material (or illusory) world and makes the laws which govern it the laws of his own being, is the will, or middle principle, and is, consequently, itself an illusion. Man's will is free in the sense that the physical world is real, and in no other. This descent into matter, or axidal coincidence of the macrocosm and the microcosm, when the former had arrived at its fourth, (or mineral) stage, therefore, took place *in equilibrio* between the two globes—(the earth and the moon) the separation of which, in the mineral kingdom, resulted from the impact of the two vortices.

This is as much as I am able to divulge in regard to the Mystery of the Eighth Sphere so far as it concerns the moon ; but I hope I have made it clear (1) that the moon is not the Eighth Sphere except in the lowest material sense, (2) that whatever of evil attaches itself to the idea of generation is mind-born and cannot be imputed to Jehovah, and (3) that what we call evil is only the cyclic law of retardation manifesting on the plane of illusion ; and that this is due to the axidal opposition of the two vortices and will disappear when their axes coincide.   It cannot be too often repeated that evil is only positive when reflected in *Maya*.   On the plane of spirit, it is simply the negation of relative good, or imperfection.   The Powers of Darkness are not in themselves evil, for they are emanations of the Divine Wisdom.   But they manifest imperfectly, because, not having completed their cycle, they are conditioned by time.   The same, however, applies to the Powers of Light who are on the *descending* arc of the cycle of Divine Love, and who manifest equally as imperfect representatives of the latter.   It is this imperfection, in itself negative, which, reflected in *Maya*, becomes antagonism, and is analogous to the darkness produced by the interference of waves of light.   But as we have seen, the two streams of tendency unite in man.   In him and through him will the universe evolve until it becomes the perfect expression of the Divine Love.   S. Paul well understood this when he said " The whole creation groaneth and travaileth in pain until now, waiting for the adoption, to wit the redemption of the body," which will take place coincidently with the manifestation (on the plane of *Maya*) of the sons of God (Rom. viii. 19).   These are the

Hindu "Agnishwatha" or Sons of Fire (pure Akâsa) which is the Sixth Principle of the cosmos. Their manifestation is the destruction of the temporal or illusory in the consuming fire of the Divine Love which, on the plane of *Maya*, is the Divine Wrath. What will happen is this. The Powers of Darkness, who can only manifest in axidal opposition, deprived of their centrifugal energy, will return to their static condition of latency. The centripetal force of the Eighth Sphere will then irresistibly draw into its vortex the residuum of material energy on globe *d*, which will then enter its first stage of "obscuration" or planetary pralâya. Of the sixteen stages of degradation which will be the lot of those whose wills have become assimilated with the material energy of the planet it is not necessary here to speak, except to say that they will be left behind in the evolutionary progress, as it were, by their own weight.

In the next lecture, I shall endeavour to show how the anomaly of the double vortex will disappear under the law of acceleration, but before leaving this part of the subject, it is necessary to add a few words on the subject of the second fall of the angels which was altogether of a different character from the first. It was a fall of the angels of light, the "sons of God" who "saw the daughters of men that they were fair" and united themselves to them in the bonds of matter. This fall from heavenly to earthly love brought them im-

mediately under the dominion of Satan, the prince of
this world, and inaugurated on earth the reign of physical and intellectual force. This union of intellect and
form was the origin of the arts and sciences. Civilization advanced by leaps and bounds, but it was a curse
rather than a blessing. By the time the fourth root
race, with its physical and intellectual giants, had
reached the apex of its development, the whole earth
was filled with violence and the great cataclysmic
period, known as the Flood, and preserved in the traditions of all nations, swept them and their children away.*
These semi-human creatures, the progeny of the
fallen angels, are known in the Hindu Scriptures as the
" Asuras " and are sometimes called " Rakshasas " or
demons, but they are quite distinct from the offspring
of the " incubi " and " succubæ " who spring from the
element of water (not, of course, material water, but
the aqueous or static principle of the universe). The
Asuras are igneous, or dynamic, in their nature, and
their power for evil was terrific. It was destroyed for
ever by the advent of Jesus Christ, and they are now,
as S. Jude puts it, " reserved in everlasting chains until the judgment (κρίσις) of the great day."†   Stated

---

* " It repented " Jehovah, lord of the Moon, " that he had made
man." Floods, earthquakes, volcanic eruptions, etc., all proceed
from the Moon.   The ebb and flow of the tides have a mysterious
connexion with life and death both in the macrocosm and the
microcosm.

† S. Jude evidently derived his knowledge of the subject from
the " Book of Enoch."

in scientific terms, they are held in check, unable to
move backwards or forwards, between the earth and
the Eighth Sphere at the point of latency, where the
attraction of both is equal on all planes, until the
"great day" of axidal coincidence, when they will be
drawn irresistibly into the vortex of the latter.   This
text in S. Jude has been unfortunately misunderstood,
and supposed to apply to Lucifer and the first fall of
the angels ; hence the Miltonic and Mediæval myths.

LECTURE VI.

SAID in a former lecture that the whole science of Occultism is built on the recognition of the reality (or permanence) of the *noumenon* and the illusory (or transitory) character of the *phenomenon*. Physical science occupies itself wholly with phenomena, and relegates noumena to the region of the unknowable. This is, however, only an intermediate phase of thought. For the last three hundred years, modern science has been developing and consolidating its *body* of phenomenal facts, and has at length arrived at a point which will necessitate a new departure in its methods ; the conclusion, viz., that force is the homogeneous basis of the material universe.

The intellectual evolution, indicated by the great scientific progress of the Post Reformation era, is the result of a spiritual *in*volutionary process which began with Augustine and ended with Calvin. For a period of intellectual renaissance is always accompanied by a spiritual decadence. It would lead me far beyond the limits assigned to this lecture if I were to endeavour to acconnt for this. Suffice it to say that it is connected with the Mystery of Birth and Death,—one of the Seven Great Mysteries* called the "Unutterable"

---

* 1. Abyss. 2. Number. 3. Affinity. 4. Birth and Death. 5. Evil. 6. The Word. 7. Godliness.

seeing that they cannot be explained in words, but necessitate the employment of a symbolical system the nature of which I am not at liberty to explain.

The spiritual involution which culminated in the worship of Force under the name of the Almighty, gave birth to inductive reasoning and inaugurated a period of intellectual evolution whose cycle is nearly completed. Determinism in theology and materialism in science have a similar origin on the plane of spirit. But a new era has begun to dawn. Neither science nor theology can rest in a *reductio ad absurdum*. The irresistible logic of Calvin was not proof againt the revolt of the moral sense, and the clearest demonstration by physiologists that mental states and moral affinities have their chemical equivalents will never persuade men to believe that " the brain secretes thought as the liver secretes bile."* This is beginning to be pretty generally recognized, and accordingly, some of our scientific men are experimenting with a view to ascertain the relations which electrical conditions, set up in the human body by the action of will, bear towards similar conditions in inorganic substances. From this it is an easy step to cosmic ideation. The mystery of force will be solved when we learn to regard it as the intermediate condition between the subjective volition and the objective act. The unmanifested idea becomes

* Attributed to the late W. K. Clifford.

manifest in the objective phenomenon through the medium of force, which may be defined, therefore, as the passage between the noumenon and the phenomenon, or the noumenon in process of manifestation. As force cannot be conceived apart from matter, or will apart from intelligence, it follows that the material universe has its origin in cosmic ideation. The recognition of this principle is tantamount to an acknowledgement of the reality or permanence of the noumenon, and when this idea has received its imprimatur at the hands of our scientists, the conflict between religion and science will come to an end, for they will have a common foundation in Sacramentalism. The Universe is, in truth, the outward and visible sign of a conflict between two eternal principles,—Light and Love, in which the noumena of all phenomena have their origin. The principles are eternal, but their conflict is temporary, hence " the fashion of this world passeth away," its archetypal forms being themselves subject to change. Evolution in the physical Universe is the sacramental expression of cosmic progress in wisdom, and beauty the sacramental index of its conformity to the Divine Ideal. But behind it lies a mysterious *Involution* of the Divine Nature which found its ultimate expression in obedience unto death,—even the Death of the Cross. And both were necessary in order that the Divine Love should become fully manifested ; for duality is an essential element of

manifestation. This is the fourth of the Seven Great
Mysteries, the " Mystery of Birth and Death." I feel
myself somewhat at a disadvantage in dealing with
this subject, for while nothing is further from my
wishes than to profane the higher mysteries, it is absolutely necessary to correct certain false notions in
regard to the relations between God and man for which
the teachings of Madame Blavatsky are responsible.
For example, nearly everyone who accepts the cosmogony of the Theosophical Society has formed a
mental picture of six globes, of a more or less gaseous
consistency, which are the companion planets of the
earth, and revolve round the sun, in the same way as
the visible planets, at a distance of so many miles from
it and from each other. Now this is entirely wrong.
No globes answering to such a description exist, at
least, as having any connection with the earth. The
fact is the seven planets are separated from the earth
and from each other, not by miles, but by inter-mole-
cular constitution. Viewed from the stand-point of the
highest consciousness in nature, or cosmic ideation, a
visible planet,—our earth for instance,—is the concrete
expression of the fourth stage of the Divine Idea
(which is complete in seven stages) or the mineral
kingdom. It contains potentially the three higher
kingdoms—and accordingly, they manifest, in connexion with it, under its own molecular law of crystallization. But the forces which held together globe "a,"

or the world of archetypal forms, were much weaker than on this earth, the *mineral idea*, so to speak having only arrived at its third stage. Plants, animals and men existed on it only in their ethereal forms. Similarly on globe " *e*," which, on the fifth " round," is the expression of the fifth stage of the Divine Idea, the mineral kingdom will enter on its period of *pralaya*, and the law of crystallization will give place to the biological law of selection when man arrives on it for the fifth time. As, in globe " *d*," the mineral idea becomes manifest on the fourth plane of consciousness, or phenomenal space (this being the fourth " round "), so the plant idea will attain to the same development on globe " *e*," in the fifth " round." In other words, man will then have entered on a period in which the recognition of his solidarity, or what is called our " common humanity," will not depend on community of flesh and blood but on community of *will*. He will exist on an altogether higher plane of consciousness, in which the illusion that the good of the individual can, by any possibility, be separated from the good of the whole will have no place. Man will have subjected to the law of his own being what I have called the *plant* idea, or the law of organic life, as, in this world, he has subjected the mineral idea, or the law of chemical affinity, which constitutes our present bond of union with each other,—our "common flesh and blood." And this community of will, consequent on the perfect development of the fifth principle in man, will be brought about by his incorporation into the sixth principle of the cosmos (Maha Buddhi) or the Christ principle. The words of S. Paul "Not I but Christ which is in me" will then express the highest form of mental activity, or the Divine Reason manifesting through the human reason.*

This digression from the subject immediately before us was necessary to clear our minds from the false notion that there is any break of continuity in man's evolution, such as the idea of a journey to another planet would imply. He does not, when he has completed his evolution on this earth, fly off into interplanetary space, as Mr. Sinnett suggests in "Esoteric Buddhism," and arrive at globe "e." He grows away from globe "d.," and into globe "e.," in the same way that he grew away from the archetypal world into that of actual form. Indeed, it would be more correct to say that the earth leaves man than that man leaves the earth; for when the fifth stage of the Divine Idea is reached, the fourth ceases to manifest, and the commencement of the fifth "round" is the first stage of "obscuration" or "planetay pralaya" of globe "d."

Thus it is that the idea of man being *on* the earth

---

* I have adopted throughout the phraseology of Madame Blavatsky, and spoken of "globes," "round" periods, etc. for the sake of convenience, but it is necessary to caution the reader against a too literal interpretation of these terms. They must not be regarded as otherwise than symbolical of the various stages of cosmic evolution.

and confined to it only holds good of his lower nature, or body of illusion. The terms higher and lower have no *real* (that is eternal) significance. The double vortex is a manifestation in time, or the plane of illusion, and is the result of cyclic aberration on the plane of spirit.

Having disposed of this fundamental error, let us endeavour to ascertain the true meaning of the account of man's creation and fall which, in the book of Genesis, is presented in the form of an allegory of so dramatic a character that it has been taken by the ignorant for a record of literal facts, with disastrous results both to religion and morality. Even where its allegorical character has been admitted, it has been grievously misinterpreted. The story of the forbidden fruit is a parable of the evolution of the human reason, and, unless we are prepared to assert that reason is in itself a bad thing, we shall do well to dismiss from our minds all poetic fictions in which the "Fall" is represented as a punishment for sin, and regard the whole story in an entirely different light.

It is not generally known that between the events described in the first and second chapters of Genesis there is an enormous interval of time :—the Elohistic Sabbath, or return of the emanations to their static condition of unmanifested latency, each being received back into the Logos in the culmination of its period. The second chapter opens with the period of Jahve-

K

Elohim, Lord of form, and ruler of the night which *preceded* the present Elohistic day, over which the Sun of Righteousness presides. An Elohistic day corresponds to what the Theosophists call a "Round" period, and this is the fourth in the new series. Jahve was, therefore, the reflection of the Divine Love on the plane of illusion. It was he who *formed* man out of the dust of the earth, and breathed into him the "*Nephesh*" or "animal soul." The purpose of this was twofold : (1) that the nascent personality might be held in equilibrium, and preserved from absorption into the Eighth Sphere, and (2) as a preparation for his future destiny of dominion over the lower kingdoms of nature ; that, through him, the universe may evolve until it becomes the perfect expression of the Divine Love. This will be better understood if we avoid the error of a time connexion between the first and second chapters of Genesis. For the first chapter embraces the whole cosmic manvantara,—the Divine Idea, from its primal differentiation in the region of the Absolute to its fullest expansion in time, or the sixth *Day* when God saw everything that he had made and behold it was very good," or more correctly, the "best" (v. 31). The first chapter of Genesis is the history of the cosmos past, present, and future, on the plane of spirit, which is now expanding into objectivity, and this expansion is a *reflexion* of the spiritual reality. Accordingly, in the second chapter, we find the order reversed. Jahve is represented as forming Adam first, and afterwards the brute creation, bringing them to him "to see what he would call them" (v. 19) and, finally, the sex principle (symbolised in the first chapter as the division of the upper and lower waters) evolves into objectivity. This is the third "Round" period of humanity, or the third Elohistic day, from *one* point of view, but it also corresponds to the minor cycle in the planetary manvantara, or the third root-race which is a microcosmic copy of it, for humanity, in the first three root-races of this "Round," repeats the process by which it evolved in the first three rounds."

I have said that the progressed entities of the former cycle (the cycle of Divine Wisdom) complete their evolution, in the new period, under the law of accleration, by incarnating in the monads who had received the breath of life (or "animal soul") from Jahve Elohim the Lord of Form, and representative of that stage of the Divine Love which, being the fourth in the series, was subject to the law of retardation. These Monads are known in India as the Seven Pitris, or Enlighteners, and are the lords of human wisdom. But though they were incarnations of the Powers of Darkness, it would be an abuse of words to call them evil, for to them man owes speech and the power to reason. By virtue of their sixth principle, which they had developed in their own cosmic manvan-

tara, they were in a position to control the fifth principle in their new condition, and awaken the dormant
faculty of reasoning in their adopted brethren.

Now the first material race (the third root race of
this " round ") were in a very real sense the first *men,*
for, though the ethereal races who preceded them had
developed will, the spiritual forces (which, manifesting
vortically downwards towards the next, or human,
plane of consciousness, were the immediate or efficient
causes of man's will) were themselves radiations from
, the Unconditioned Cause—the Divine Will. Man was
a mere image or reflexion of God, and his will an illusion, a shadow of the Divine Will projected in Maya.
Not until the fourth " round," was the human personality, so to speak, *born,* or detached from the life of its
parents the Elohim. Man, to have an independent
existence, must be self-centred, or free to originate his
own actions, and it is evident that this could not be if
the evolution of his reason had proceeded on the same
lines. Hence the necessity for a re-adjustment whereby his personality, or fifth principle, might become itself a controlling impulse. The mystery of free-will is,
in truth, the mystery of human personality, and this,
as we have seen, has its source in the Divine Love,
which requires an object in order that it may become
manifest. We can only conceive of will as the dynamic
effect of personality manifesting objectively. In itself it
has no existence, for it is neither subject nor object but

a middle category necessitated by the laws of thought. In all finite personalities the will is the centre of gravity,—a mathematical point. In God, the Infinite Personality, there is no centre, or rather the centre is everywhere, for in Him subjective and objective are One, and, in manifestation, both comprehend all that is. It is easy to see, therefore, that the projection of will in *Maya* must be accompanied by a projection of *mayavic* personality in order that it may become manifest, or present an objective side. The centre must be located; hence the apparent opposition between the will of man and the Will of God. As the Will of God is the centre from which force radiates, passing in turn through every plane of consciousness, this apparent opposition will disappear when the personality, or fifth principle, of man shall be sufficiently developed to obtain full control over the forces which have thrown into objectivity his lower principles, and which have resulted in the anomaly of the double vortex,—an anomaly because its centre resides in the fourth, or illusory, principle corresponding to the fourth, or mayavic, stage of the Divine Idea concerning him.

Our investigations have therefore led us to this point; that man, as he is at present constituted, is the resultant of two vortices manifesting dynamically on the plane of illusion, and proceeding originally from two separate streams of tendency, the one representing Divine Love, and the other, the Divine Wisdom, which, meeting on the plane of human consciousness, coalesce into an objective personality, imperfect as a reflexion of the Divine Personality, inasmuch as its centre is located in maya. This imperfection is due to a disturbance of the medium through which it manifests and is the temporary result of the impact of the two vortices, as the reflexion of a light in water is duplicated when the surface is disturbed.

It is desirable here to anticipate an objection which may be raised to this illustration. Why, it may be said, should the term " *maya* " be applied to the fourth stage of the Evolutionary series in the macrocosm when it may be predicated equally of the whole series? The answer is to be found in the etymology of the word. It is a contraction of "maha-aya." "Ya" signifies being, " a " is the privative particle and " maha" is "great." "Maya" therefore signifies "the Great Is Not." But the term "great" is relative, and applies to the objective universe on each plane of consciousness. We may therefore speak of maya *in its fourth degree* which is the Universe of *form*, or all that pertains to three-dimensional space and is limited by time. It is in this sense that I use the word for our present illustration.

But though, from a metaphysical point of view, we may regard the objective universe as mayavic, yet it has for us a real existence, inasmuch as our human personality is still within the sphere of its attraction. The first step towards the recognition of its true character, as essentially illusory, will be taken when man shall have sufficiently developed his fifth principle to enable him to overcome this attraction,—in other words, when the centrifugal force of his lower nature shall become subject to the centripetal force of his higher nature. At present they are *in equilibrio* in the average man for all practical purposes, though, in comparing individuals, we may observe a slight preponderance one way or the other. When the centripetal preponderance is very marked the individual is regarded by the majority as a visionary enthusiast or a dangerous fanatic. When, on the other hand, the animal nature is not under proper control the human beast must be caged in the interests of society.* Until the divine reflexion has recovered from the shock produced in its medium by the impact of the two vortices, man must continue to manifest as a double vortex with a centre of its own. But it is easy to see that this condition cannot be otherwise than temporary. The law of acceleration which enabled the Powers of Darkness to traverse successfully the manifestation of the Divine Love on the plane of illusion, by opposing to it their own more rapid vortex, must necessarily give place to the law of retardation in the new figure thus thrown into objectivity. Having exhausted itself in the centri-

---

* The reader must be careful to distinguish between the *real* centre which resides in the fifth principle and the *mayavic* centre of the fourth which we call will.

fugal impulse which gave birth to the Eighth Sphere, and, in the mineral kingdom, was the cause of the moon becoming a satellite of the earth*, the tendency of the vortex is to return to its static condition of latency, which tendency manifests *dynamically* in the attraction of the Eighth Sphere. On the other hand, the Dhyanis, proceeding from the Elohim of Light, who descended into matter, under the cyclic law of re-tardation, began to ascend immediately afterwards. The law of acceleration then asserted itself, and by the time that the fourth root race had reached the apex of its development, was sufficiently powerful to success-fully resist the attraction of the Eighth Sphere, and preserve the double vortex from absorption into it. This is one aspect of the law of cataclysms, referred to in " Esoteric Buddhism," which are as periodic as the swing of a pendulum. They occur at the end of every " root race " because the Principalities (or angels of periods) of the succeeding one are then evolving at their minimum rate, having completed one-half of their minor cycle.—At such times, the centripetal resistance to the attraction of the Eighth Sphere is at its weakest. These periods coincide with the precession of the

---

* The relations of the earth and the moon correspond, in the macrocosm, to the double vortex which is the symbol of the higher and lower nature in man. The correspondence is so precise that the author regrets his inability (for reasons which will be obvious to every initiate) to illustrate it in detail.

equinoxes, the last was the end of the glacial epoch in the northern hemisphere, and is preserved in the memory of a universal flood in the traditions of all nations. But it is with the preceding cataclysm in the third root race that we are now concerned ; called by theologians the " Fall," and by the occultists, the " Descent into Matter." It is symbolised in the book of Genesis as expulsion from Paradise,—(rest, or spiritual equilibrium) and the curse pronounced on the earth for man's sake was not the arbitrary decree of an offended Deity, but the natural and inevitable result of the shock, caused by the impact of the vortices, which brought all lower forms of life within the attraction of the Eighth Sphere, and, consequently, under lunar influences. It was coincident with the evolution of sex ; hence it is often called the " Fall into generation," the phenomena of gestation and parturition being intimately connected with lunar phases and following the course of lunar cycles. The races which preceded what Madame Blavatsky calls the " Lemuro-Atlanteans " were differently constituted from later man, and reproduced themselves by a law analogous to that which governs the production of materialized forms in the " spirit-circle," with this important difference,—that the form was permanent, or, at least, persistent.

With the fall into generation man became subject to the law of heredity, and this is the foundation of the much misunderstood doctrine of "original sin" which, according to its popular interpretation, is a monstrous libel on the Divine Being. Had man not fallen into generation, the Divine Purpose concerning him would not have been fulfilled. On the one hand, the double vortex would have been absorbed in the Eighth Sphere, or on the other, the principalities of Light would have infused into him a portion of their own spiritual essence and caused him to evolve rapidly, under the law of acceleration, out of materiality into a state of pure and self-dependent spiritual existence. In the one case his material, and in the other, his spiritual personality would have been destroyed. But the principalities of Light, perfect and blessed emanations of the Divine Wisdom, recognized in the Divine Love a Purpose above and beyond anything that the highest wisdom could attain to. It was no less than the redemption of the body by sacrifice, and before this Mystery, they cast their crowns of wisdom at the feet of the Mystic Lamb, and veiled their faces in adoration. They might have redeemed man's soul, they could not redeem his body. Accordingly, they submitted to the law of their cycle, and became angels of periods, each period being a progressive manifestation of the Divine Love which was to prepare the way for its perfect manifestation in the WORD MADE FLESH.

Now the period of the Jewish dispensation, or that ruled over by the principalities proceeding from Jahve,

lord of form, was essentially the period of *generation.*
It had for its object the consolidation of humanity on
the basis of that sympathetic relation which we call
"natural affection," in order that, through it, man might
rise to the conception of the Divine Fatherhood. Accordingly, the solidarity of the human race found its
natural expression in that community of feeling in
which we recognize our essential brotherhood, and also
in the law of inherited tendencies by which the equilibrium of the double vortex is preserved. Against this
law the principalities of Darkness, under the guidance
of Lucifer (prince of this world), have opposed their
most powerful forces, but, as we shall see, with only
partial success. It is generally supposed that Satan is
the enemy of spirituality in man ; that he delights in
his degradation, and views with diabolical (?) satisfaction the development of his lower nature and all its
evil consequences. The wide, and almost universal,
prevalence of this mediæval superstition only makes it
all the more necessary to protest against it as a grotesque
error. As well might we say that the object at which
Napoleon aimed was the slaughter of as many French
soldiers as possible. It is related of Napoleon that he
wept bitterly when, on the night succeeding the battle
of Austerlitz, he rode over the field and viewed the dead
and dying,—and it would probably be much nearer the
truth to say that the degradation and suffering of mankind, for which the adversary of God is responsible, so

far from affording him any satisfaction, afflicts him with a sense of failure and deepens his despair of ultimate victory.

Let us examine this "*diabolical*" delusion in the light of revelation and common sense.   How can any rational being delight in evil for its own sake? Such delight is the negation of rationality, and the nearest approach to such a conception is the homicidal maniac.   It is admitted that Satan is not only a rational being, but an intelligence of a far higher order than our own.   To suppose, therefore, that his chief characteristic is insensate ferocity is surely absurd. Without, of course, pressing the analogy, if we were compelled to choose between Napoleon the Great and the Whitechapel murderer as a representative of the usurping Prince of this world, nobody who reflects for a moment would hesitate, not even those who call the latter a "fiend in human shape."

If we turn to revelation what do we find?   S. Peter, it is true, compares him to a "roaring lion seeking whom he may devour," or in other words, whose nature he may *assimilate* to his own.   He is also called the "father of lies," or illusions, for it was through his instrumentality that man's personality came under the dominion of *maya.*   Everywhere else he is the symbol of pure cold intellect.   In the book of Job, the oldest extant dramatic allegory, he is represented as the author of the cynical assertion that love is only a form

of self-interest, and we are left to imagine his astonishment at the words of Job—" Though He slay me, yet
will I trust in Him." In the genetic allegory he is
symbolised as the serpent,—everywhere the emblem
of wisdom,—and *enlightenment* was the immediate
consequence of eating the forbidden fruit. He is, in
fact, Lucifer the light-bearer, and to him man owes the
faculty of intellectual discrimination, or the knowledge
of good and evil under illusory conditions.* He is the
manifestation, *in time*, of the fifth, or intellectual, principle of the cosmos, and in virtue of this limitation, is
incapable of conceiving any higher good than wisdom.
We must be careful, however, to distinguish between
the seven cosmic principles and their microcosmic
manifestations, each of which is a complete sub-series.

---

* The definition of good as the "greatest happiness of the
greatest number" is purely Satanic in its implied assumption that
evil is the happiness of the fewer, and, consequently, that evil and
happiness are capable of being connoted.   That such a definition
should pass muster in a "Christian" nation shews how immeasurably inferior, as a philosophical system, is modern Christianity to
the "heathen" philosophy of Plato.   It must be apparent to every
reader of the Protagoras that good and pleasure, evil and pain,
are not interchangeable values, and must be weighed, so to speak
in different scales.   The perception of harmony and discord, which
has its foundation in the eternal principle of number, or infinity
manifesting through progress, is alone capable of furnishing a
standard of value to which good and evil may be referred.   For
the spiritual degradation which hinders man from disconnecting
good with pleasure and evil with pain, Lucifer is responsible, but
this is the *result* of his opposition and not the motive which induced
him to traverse the Divine Purpose.

Thus, Lucifer is a fully-developed septenary being, representing the fifth principle of the Universe, or cosmic ideation, and striving to attain to omnipotence through control of the fourth *(maha maya)*. Now this is not spiritual evolution, or life, as, at first sight, it might appear, but *involution*, or the spiritual principle of death. This is exceedingly difficult to explain, but it must be remembered that evolution is progress in *time*, and is the reflexion in maya of a spiritual reality which is not so conditioned. Lucifer is not the fifth cosmic principle itself, but its efflorescence in time. He is the seed of the fifth human principle, and germination is an involutionary process as regards the seed itself, (except a corn of wheat fall into the ground *and die* it bringeth forth no fruit) though evolutionary as regards the nascent plant. This view is quite in accordance with our original position that evil has no real¹ (*i.e.*, eternal) existence, but is an imperfect, or lower, goodness.

What, then, was the design which the author of evil on this planet set himself to accomplish ? It was no less than the elevation of man to his own spiritual level, in order that, through him, the cosmos might become the perfect expression of pure intellect. It was a magnificent ideal worthy of a son of light, but it was doomed to failure. A yet higher glory was in store for man. He was destined for adoption, that, becoming a partaker of the Divine

Nature, the Universe, through him, might evolve into the perfect expression of Love, or God Himself. Accordingly, the light-bearer found himself confronted with a law of inertia sufficiently powerful to resist even his mighty will. His labours resemble those of Sisyphus. Having united his fate with man, his future is bound up with man's intellectual progress, and this is subject to a rhythmical cyclic and sub-cyclic ebb and flow, consequent on the periodic law of acceleration and retardation. It baffles his utmost efforts, and is the cause of that strange oscillation between the positive and negative poles of spiritual wisdom which, reflected in *maya*, is the conflict of good and evil. But this antagonism is essential to the perfect revelation of the Divine Nature, or in other words, the omnipotence of Love. That God is Love is no oriental metaphor, but a plain literal statement containing the key to all mysteries. The existence of evil, it is often said, is a proof that either the goodness or the power of God is limited. We refuse to impale ourselves on either horns of the dilemma. The existence of evil is a proof that God is not Will or Wisdom but Love. If the omnipotence of God were displayed in His Will, there could be no freedom, and, consequently, no personality for the creature. If wisdom were the highest good, an immeasurable chasm would for ever have separated the creature from the Creator—for the most exalted spiritual condition is only a form of life, excluding of necessity all lower forms, and proceeding from the Lord and Giver of *all* life.*

But God has chosen to reveal Himself as Love, hence the necessity of freedom on the part or man to choose between good and evil, for, were he not free, he would be incapable of reciprocating that love.

Here, however, we are met by a difficulty. All material effects have their origin in spiritual causes, and we have seen that positive evil on the material plane is the result of cyclic aberration on the plane of spirit, consequent on the impact of two vortical streams of tendency, producing a disturbance in the medium through which the human consciousness manifests objectively. Thus it is that the fifth principle, or seat of human personality, is subject to a periodic cyclic and subcyclic law of attraction toward the fourth or "body of desire" which, owing to its own imperfect development, it is incapable of fully controlling. But the question arises,—if this attraction towards the lower nature or "body of desire" is the cause of suffering and death

---

* If we regard all forms of life as rays proceeding from the One Centre, God the Father, the energizing Influence is the Lord and Giver of life, the Holy Ghost,—and its Perfect Expression, the Son "begotten of His Father *before* all worlds,"—"Light of light" or the Divine Wisdom, the highest form of life. But, as the line revolving on its axis produces the circle, so does the circle produce the Sphere, the Divine Wisdom coming into relation with life at every point. He is thus God of God or the Perfect Expression of the Divine Love in its outward manifestation, and "by Him were all things made."

must it not be considered as in itself an evil condition? By no means ; for it produces also pleasure and life, which we can only know by their opposites, and secondly, pleasure and pain are only finite correlatives of the eternal principles of good and evil. It is against this law of inertia in the double vortex that the adversary of God and man rebels. In vain does he attempt to detach the fifth principle from the body of desire, and assimilate it to the fifth principle of the cosmos to which he himself belongs. The fall into generation has preserved the equilibrium between the fourth and the eighth sphere, and the orderly cyclic path of man's intellectual evolution. It is the human law of gravity, and corresponds to the centripetal force by which the planet holds its satellite in subjection. We may regard it in two aspects ; as the cause of "original sin," and the effect of the Divine Love.

Now original sin, as I have said, is neither more nor less than the "law of heredity." However much we may dislike it, the fact remains that man has an animal nature, with passions and instincts that link him on one side of his being with the brutes that perish. He is also conscious that he occupies an anomalous position in the Universe, for while the gratifications of sense afford entire satisfaction to the brute creation, they can never, refine them as he may, constitute happiness for him. At the same time they are a hindrance to the development of his higher nature, so that, re-

L

garded simply from an intellectual point of view, they are an intolerable nuisance. The pursuit of knowledge is checked by continual temptations, more or less alluring, to forsake a path so beset with thorns and " gather rosebuds while we may" and the distant view is bounded by the horizon of death.

Until we know the *meaning* of life, the question will ever obtrude itself whether, after all, it be worth living. Now all religions profess to solve this problem, and the religion of a nation or race is a fair index of its intellectual and spiritual development. Wherever a purely Aryan, or a purely Semitic, type prevails, both show a strong tendency to degenerate. An example of the former may be observed in India where the intellectual element has degenerated into the grossest superstition and nature-worship, and of the latter, in Mahommedan countries, where the spiritual monotheistic element has become the crudest anthropomorphism. And, in Christian countries, where either element has unduly prevailed, and overlaid or corrupted the Catholic faith, there, on the one hand, flourish devotional puerilities, or, on the other, a peculiarly repulsive form of Protestantism which is the death of true spirituality. It is the Nemesis of all false or defective systems of religion that they fail most signally in the very purpose for which they were instituted,—that of elevating humanity, and the reason is that they are one and all based on the fundamentally unsound proposition that the body is, not the servant, but the *enemy* of the soul.

This error has its source in ignorance of the fact that man was created, not for himself, but for the glory of God, and we shall endeavour to trace it to its fountain-head.

We have now arrived at a point from which we can view without prejudice the spiritual antagonism which is the Origin of Evil. It is a negative principle. Absolute evil is nothing, absolute good is God or Love. All that is, is more or less good compared with non-being, and more or less evil compared with God ; and the spiritual activities of Lucifer are of the nature of a lower good in conflict with a higher.   In order to understand it we must take into consideration two very important facts (1) that the element of will, essential to the idea of conflict which, on the plane of human consciousness, is of the nature of a Cause, on the plane of spiritual consciousness, is of the nature of an Effect.   In other words, where the one ends the other begins.   And (2) we must remember that the Fall of the Angels was a fall from heavenly to earthly wisdom. It was spiritual death, and as death is always followed by birth, their fall was the re-birth of intelligence on the plane of human consciousness.   All forms of material activity have their origin on the plane of spirit, and all forms of spiritual activity may be divided into synthetic, or constructive, and analytic, or destructive. Both have their place in the economy of the Universe, and neither are, in themselves, good or evil, high or low.

Now the spiritual activities of Jahve are synthetic or formative. His period (the period of Jehovah-Michael) is the time connexion between the Father and Mother principles in Nature, and it culminated in the manifestation of the Word made Flesh. He is the " Lord of Sabaoth " or the Dhyan Chohanic hosts of Light who are on the descending arc of their cycle, and preside over what are called " natural forces" Individually will-less, they represent collectively the Divine Will and the harmony of their diverse operations constitutes the Divine Providence. The Captain of these hosts is Michael (Heb. " like unto God) and he is represented in the book of "Revelations" as prevailing against the Dragon, that ancient symbol of wisdom, and casting him out of heaven, not into a mythical hell, but *into the earth*, and his angels with him. Henceforward " their place was found no more in heaven," and the angels of light became angels of darkness, groping in Maya—the great abyss, or bottomless pit. The light that was in them became the property of man. It raised him from a mere automaton into a reasonable creature, capable of reciprocating the Divine Love, and of intelligent co-operation with the Divine Purpose concerning him.

Thus we see that the " Fall " of the Angels was

overruled for man's benefit, and that, while it may be truly said to be the *origin* of evil, it was not *in itself* evil, but part of a grand scheme whereby man, by attaining to self-consciousness through experience, might become worthy of adoption, and, partaking of the Divine Nature, manifest in person the Omnipotence of Love.* Let us remember that evil is nothing but failure of adaptation to environment, and that the Love of God is the environment of Being on every plane of consciousness. We can only, as Hegel points out, conceive of being as *becoming*, and for this cause the whole creation groaneth and travaileth in pain (the pangs of imperfection,—a necessary element in time manifestation) waiting for the adoption.

The story of the " Fall " in the book of Genesis is an allegorical presentment of a conflict which, originating on the plane of spirit, and issuing through the gates of Maya, entered the plane of human consciousness, and gave birth to the Mayavic opposition between the will of man and the Will of God. The symbol of the conflict is the double vortex with its equilibrated centre between the Fourth and the Eighth Sphere and we can thus see that, while evil arises from the human will, the freedom which renders it possible can in no real sense be regarded as its cause. We are, therefore, in a better position to understand the nature

---

* Love cannot be *fully* manifested towards the perfect.

of the conflict whose issues regulate every department
of human activity in the mass and determine the
course of human history, inasmuch as it secures for
each individual that freedom of will which enables
him to co-operate with the Powers of either light or
darkness, and, to a greater or less degree, hasten or
retard the fulfilment of the Divine Purpose. In a very
real sense, therefore, we may be said to wrestle with
Principalities and Powers, and the Rulers of the darkness of this world (αιων) and spiritual wickedness in
the celestial region (Eph. vi. 12), for it is only through
and by means of the human will that these can manifest on the plane of human consciousness.

From these facts we may deduce the following conclusions (1) that the Fall of the Angels was not caused
by their "rebellious will," but that the rebellious will
of man had its origin in the imperfect control which
the new-born intelligence exercised over his lower
nature, and (2) that the spiritual conditions under
which the higher and lower nature respectively developed were mutually antagonistic ; the one deriving
its vitality from the synthetic, or formative, activity on
the plane of spirit, and the other resulting from dis-
criminatory, or analytic, spiritual activity.

This being premised, we have now to consider the
part played by the reason in bringing about the disor-
ganisation of human activity which is the cause of evil
n the world.   It must not be forgotten that the intel-

lectual faculty is essentially *analytic*, and that the power of *synthesis* belongs to the sixth principle. And here it is necessary to correct an error into which many Theosophists have fallen. They have taken it for granted that the power to reason resides wholly in the fifth principle because it is the vehicle of the human, as distinguished from the animal, personality. The mistake has probably arisen from the very materialistic view of the seven principles set forth in " Esoteric Buddhism " in which each one is treated of separately as if it were an independent entity.* Now while it is true that the power to *discriminate*, resides in the fifth principle, and is accordingly possessed, in a greater or less degree, by the brute creation, whose fourth principle, or body of desire is thereby controlled ; the power to *reason*, which involves synthetisation of disconnected concepts has its origin in the embryotic sixth principle. As the lower animals would be mere automata without the faculty of discrimination, so would man be wholly destitute of responsibility towards God and his fellow-man, were he incapable of synthetising to some degree his relations towards them.

Now the sixth principle in man corresponds to the sixth principle of the Cosmos or the Divine Wisdom,

---

* Mr. Mohini M. Chatterjee, a Hindu Theosophist, has characterised this treatment as responsible for the doctrine that man is like "a very complicated onion from which coat after coat may be peeled until nothing is left." See " Man : Fragments of forgotten history." By Two Chelas.

"Who for us men and for our Salvation" entered the great Abyss of Maya and in process of time, manifested in the Flesh and was born of a pure Virgin. He was made manifest in order that he might "destroy the works of the Devil" or the Elohim of Darkness, who are, collectively, the fifth cosmic principle, and whose efflorescence in time is Satan the Adversary.

Without entering into futher details, we may take our stand on the broad principle that the Divine Love, which operates on every plane of human consciousness as the Vivifier and Sustainer, is opposed by the involutionary forces which originate in the spiritual activities of a being who was formerly a Son of Light but who has been plunged into the Abyss of Maya.

Satan is, therefore, on the material plane, the author of disease and physical death, of falsehood on the intellectual plane, and on the plane of spirit, selfishness, or the negation of Love. For all that, he is a minister of God, fulfilling the Divine Purpose by this very opposition, without which the omnipotence of Love could not become manifest. To him Love is a consuming fire, and the Divine Wisdom a great horror of darkness. He and his legions are fighting for their lives and have intrenched themselves in the human personality, as in a fortress, from whence Love and Love only can drive them.

We see, therefore, that it was Love which drove man from Paradise to the earth, and called into existence free-will by attaching his fourth principle, or body of desire, to the earth by a bond sufficiently strong to balance the centrifugal impetus. Up to the time when he began to develope intelligence, the action of man's will had been purely automatic, the plane of its energies, so to speak, coinciding with the axis of the original vortex. But in the newly-objectivised double vortex, the lower nature required to be consolidated in order to preserve it from absorption into the Eighth Sphere. Free-will in man may therefore be defined as the point of equilibrium between his fifth, or intellectual principle, and his fourth, or body of desire. Man thus became a responsible being with faculties capable of adapting themselves to the law of Love which called him into existence. He is the seed of the Divine Love fructifying in the womb of Maya the great Abyss, or the *Illusion of the Is-not* made pregnant by the Divine Love. This is the Mystery of mysteries which no wisdom of the creature can ever fathom, but which was revealed (though "as in a glass darkly") when the Word became Flesh and dwelt among us. He took on Himself a body that He might redeem our bodies by grafting them with His own in order that the Universe might become the perfect expression of the Divine Love.

On the question of Sacramentalism I can touch but briefly. It is the assertion of the principle that matter is the vehicle of spirit, and its recognition is an intel-

lectual necessity if we are to make any further progress towards comprehension of the natural order.
The Sacraments are seven in number,—Baptism, Confirmation, Eucharist, Matrimony, Penance, Order and
Extreme Unction. They are the *evolutionary* equivalents of the sevenfold *involutionary* spiritual energy
which in the natural order, cause the phenomena of
Birth, Strength, Nutrition, Generation, Recuperation,
Speech and Transmutation. Conversely, they stand
to man's lower nature in the relation of Death to Sin,
Weakness to the Flesh, Absorption in the Higher,
Self-Surrender, Mortification, Obedience and Adaptation. The dynamic effects, therefore (if we may use
the expression), of the Christian Sacraments are *involutionary* as regards the lower and *evolutionary* in
respect to the higher nature of man. If we apply
this idea to the symbol of the double vortex, we shall
recognize in the Sacraments the appointed means
whereby the opposing forces will ultimately range
themselves around their true centre,—the personality
(the fifth or human principle) and the attraction of
the Eighth Sphere be neutralized. The spheroidal
vortices will then coalesce and become one, first as an
elliptical spheroid and afterwards as a true sphere
capable of indefinite expansion.

Sacramentalism is the assertion of a principle which
has its analogy in nature in every case where a lower
type of life is succeeded by a higher one. As F. D.

Maurice points out, "it assumes Christ to be the Lord, it assumes that men are created *in Him*,— that this is the constitution of our race ; that therefore all attempts of men to resolve themselves into separate units are contradictory and abortive."*

In bringing this course of lectures to an end I may say that it has been my endeavour to supply materials whereby the true gnosis may be distinguished from the "oppositions of science falsely so called." The agnosticism which is the characteristic of modern thought is an indication that the times are ripe for imparting truths which, twenty years ago, would have been as seed falling on the wayside. The remedy for evils which spring from ignorance is knowledge, but until the ignorance is confessed, the remedy cannot be. applied. So long as men were satisfied with mechanical authority in religion ; so long as it was considered scientific to call the unknown the Unknowable ; in other words, while men preferred darkness to light nothing could be done. But we have lately witnessed a reaction from agnosticism and a revival of gnosticism in one of its most dangerous forms. It is, therefore, of the highest importance that we should learn to distinguish the truths to which it bears witness from the falsehoods with which they have been artfully blended.

---

* The Kingdom of Christ. Vol. I. p. 326.

APPENDIX TO LECTURE I.

SINCE these lectures were delivered, the "Reminiscences of H. P. Blavatsky by the Countess Wachtmeister and others" have appeared. Taken in conjunction with what is known of her career prior to the formation of the Theosophical Society, they tend strongly to confirm the view that she was exploited by different persons at different periods.

On page 57, for example, the Countess relates how she saw "in a scrap-book in faded writing" dated 1851 a few lines in Madame Blavatsky's handwriting describing her first interview with " The Master."

> " Nuit memorable : certaine nuit par un clair de lune qui se couchait à Ramsgate (*videlicet* Hyde Park) 12th Août 1851— lorsque je rencontrai le Maître de mes rêves."

This, it seems, was an "immensely tall" Hindu whom Countess Wachtmeister remembers hearing of as having accompanied some Indian princes that year on an "important mission" to this country,—probably a visit to the great Exhibition. Whether it was "Koot Hoomi" or the more shadowy " Mahatma M——" of the " Occult world" (since identified as a name-sake of Madame Blavatsky's old nurse Marya) we are not told, but the individual in question "required her co-operation in a work he was about to undertake," and suggested that she should found the Theosophical Society. He "told her that she would have to spend three years in Thibet to prepare her for the important task," and accordingly " H. P. Blavatsky decided to accept the offer made to her, and shortly afterwards left London for India," presumably for initiation into the mysteries of the "Ancient Wisdom Religion."

Now we know from Colonel Olcott's " People from the other World" that in 1874 Madame Blavatsky's " Master " (or control) professed himself to be the "spirit" of a bold buccaneer called John King who flourished in the seventeenth century and amused himself in the nineteenth by " precipitating " letters (page 455) and fetching medals of honour from the coffin of Madame Blavatsky's father (page 355). Moreover it was Colonel Olcott himself who first suggested that " John King" was no deceased buccaneer but the creation of an " Order which, while depending for its results upon unseen agents, has its existence upon earth amongst men " (page 454).

It must have been shortly after this that the " Koot Hoomi " delusion was born, for in 1879 we find him " precipitating " letters to Mr. Sinnett, and instructing him in the Elements of " Esoteric Buddhism " which was suddenly sprung upon the Theosophical Society, and nearly caused a schism between its Eastern and Western branches.

The "Kiddle incident" took place early in 1883 and Madame Blavatsky, now completely at liberty, set about repairing the breaches which "Koot Hoomi" had made. The "Reminiscences" contain (page 114) an extract from the "Path" in which two mysterious certificates are given having reference to the authorship of the Secret Doctrine. It is not very difficult to read between the lines of Dr. Hübbe Schleiden's account that "Koot Hoomi" claims to have a finger in the pie. But the fact that Dr. Schleiden saw "a good deal of the well-known blue Koot Hoomi handwriting" while the Secret Doctrine was in progress, is by no means a proof that Madame Blavatsky was still under his influence.   Every Spiritualist knows that identity of handwriting does not necessarily imply identity of control.   The whole affair is very puzzling, and it is doubtful whether even Madame Blavatsky herself could at all times distinguish between what was original and what was dictated, still less how far "John King" was responsible for the latter and how far the "Mahâtmas."

When we consider, however, that one of the conditions on which her release from "prison" was obtained was that the Hindu Brothers of the Left, who wished to make use of her, should not interfere with anything that had already taken place, we can understand that the Kiddle fiasco would only have the effect of throwing her back on her original controls.   She might still beieve in the Thibetan source of her inspirations, and on this point she could not be undeceived, owing to the terms of the compromise, though it must have been gall and worm-wood to her Hindu friends. Accordingly, it was only necessary for her to re-christen "John King," and confer brevet rank upon the "spirit" of her old nurse Marya, known afterwards as "Mahâtma *Morya*," as Smith becomes "Smythe" when he rises in the world. How far Madame Blavatsky was herself responsible for this deception, or indeed, whether she was responsible at all, it is difficult to say, and the question is still further complicated if we take into account the evident signs of dual personality which she exhibited. It "needs no ghost" (or Mahâtma) to account, for example, for her sudden change of mind at Würtzburg respecting Countess Wachtmeister's visit. Madame Blavatsky would have preferred her room to her company, but "H.P.B." could not do without her. She had seen clairvoyantly a manuscript album in her possession and required it immediately.

But let us set against all her tricks, conscious, or unconscious, the story of the poor woman and the steerage tickets related on page 147 of the "Reminiscences," and remember that far worse sins than Madame Blavatsky was ever accused of were pardoned in one who, like her, "loved much." R.I.P.

CPSIA information can be obtained
at www.ICGtesting.com
Printed in the USA
LVHW010430180119
604384LV00019B/701/P